Genesis 1-2-3

Creation: Then and Now

Dwight O. Troyer

Contents

Dedication

I dedicate this book to . . .

Teresa, who taught me how to love, and be a better person.

My children—Nate, Brent, John, Matthew, and Genevieve—who have not had an easy road to travel because of unusual circumstances in their individual lives, and I love them all.

My father Oliver M Troyer Jr.: for his love of life and his desire to live. On June 28, 2007, at the good old age of eighty-nine, he went home to be with Jesus.

My mother Pauline, who loves unconditionally all who are close to her and has been a wonderful inspiration to everyone in the way that she has cared for my dad for sixty-three years through very tough situations. What a lady!

My sister Jo Anne whom God has called to excellence in all she does.

My weight lifting friend John Donovan, we have been through much together. Through it all, no matter what has come, I have been able to call him a friend and a brother.

My spiritual father Kenneth E. Hagin for all he has planted in my life and his faithfulness to his call from God.

My pastor John King, an obedient servant, who inspires me to be the best that I can be for God and demonstrates obedience to God's voice that is rare in this time and hour.

Everybody who has affected me in a bad way or a good way, because you have helped squeeze and shape me into the person I am today. To the people I have failed, taken advantage of, lied to, spoken badly about, or sinned against in any other way, please forgive me! I hope when you read this book, you can see God's mercy and grace to all of us. If God can use me as bad as I have been to you, just think of the miracles He can do through you.

Keep looking up! Jesus is coming soon!

Introduction

Life was good! My name is Dwight Oliver Troyer, but most of the people I knew called me Ollie. I owned a bar and restaurant called Ollie's in the small town of Hopedale, Illinois. I opened the bar around 8:00 A.M. every morning. I closed it almost every night around 12:00 P.M. to 1:00 A.M. The town was pretty flexible with me and gave me latitude to stay open later if the customers were there. We served noon meals Monday through Friday. We also served suppers Wednesday, Friday, and Saturday nights. My life was set and I was happy. I was motivated by the money and thought I would run this business until I retired. I had owned the bar for eight years, part of the time with my dad, and I had just turned thirty years old. I was driving north on route 121 in Illinois, north of Tremont, just approaching the edge of Morton. The road was a two-lane highway, which was about to expand into a four-lane highway. Bob Grimm Chevrolet was just to the right of the highway beside the Fields Shopping Center. Suddenly it happened! This moment would change my life forever. There was a U-turn at that time in my life, and I didn't see it coming. I slammed head-on into the truth even though I didn't realize the magnitude of what was about to happen to me.

My thoughts were full of lust, and I was happy to have this free time. I was thinking about every one of the bars I was going to stop at, and I was fantasizing about them. When suddenly I was a little child in my thoughts, and I saw and heard my mother tell me, "Someday you will pick a church." It was like I saw a mini-vision of an instant in my childhood. Immediately I began to think, "How could I pick a church? What do I know about church?" Then it happened! A male voice spoke to me from nowhere. It oozed with love and was gentle, but it had power and authority behind it like the sound of Niagara Falls. Words cannot explain the sound of that voice. Tears come to my eyes as I remember the moment when God spoke to me. As bad as I was, doing what I was doing, God spoke. His voice said three words that changed my life forever, "Buy a Bible!" The instant that happened, I saw another vision of the front of Boyd's Christian Bookstore in the Fields Shopping Center. All of this happened in an instant or a moment in time. Now the voice of God was echoing in my consciousness. I began to feel like I was going to die if I didn't obey the voice and buy a Bible. I drove on to Peoria, but my thoughts had now changed from lust to fear. I went to a store called Sidney Harrison and picked up a couple of cases of drinking glasses for the bar, along with three or four shot glasses and different items needed to restock my supply for the bar and restaurant. My direction in life had begun to change even though I didn't realize it.

So there I was with all of the things I needed to run the business purchased. I threw them in the truck and drove straight back to Boyd's Christian Bookstore. I walked in and walked up to the counter and said, "I want to buy someone a Bible. What do you recommend?" A tiny-framed, gentle young lady smiled and said, "What type of Bible would you like?" This question made me a little uneasy because I didn't know how to respond. I had never purchased a Bible before and had never given any thought to them. I knew nothing about Bibles. I thought they were something you bought and put on a table for display purposes. The idea of reading one had never really crossed my mind. My mother had a Bible, but I could never remember her reading it. My father never went to church, therefore why would I? I was a self-proclaimed agnostic, meaning I believed there was a God but I thought it foolish for anybody to say their way was the only way. I mean, look at all of the religions: Muslims, Hindus, Jews, Jehovah's Witnesses, Christians, and many more. Everybody believes his or her way to be the truth. When I was in the army, I had no preference placed on my dog tags for religious affiliation because I didn't believe any religion was better or worse than another.

Now here I was buying a Bible because I heard this voice say, "Buy a Bible!" I felt out of place to say the least. I had not responded back to woman at the sales counter because I didn't know what to say. Purchasing a Bible was new to me. So she genteelly asked, "Who is it for?" Now I was really in a mess on the inside, and all I wanted to do was get a Bible and get out of this creepy store. Who would come into a Christian bookstore anyway? The only reason I was there was because I had heard this voice and I was going to obey it so I didn't die. I fumbled for words, "What difference does that make?" I was not about to tell anybody I heard a voice say, "Buy a Bible!" They would think I was nuts. I mean, I would have thought somebody was crazy if they had told me that. The difference was that I had heard the voice. I wasn't drinking. And I knew what just happened to me doesn't happen to people. Therefore, I was not going to tell anybody. I stayed cool, settled down, and asked, "What do you recommend?"

She spewed out a litany of stuff I did not understand about Bibles. So I just stood there and took it all in. She said something about a King James Bible. I had heard this terminology before somewhere. Someone had talked about this

Bible in a conversation, "The King James Bible is the only true Bible." I never knew what the person meant by that, but I didn't really care at the time. The woman went on and said, "A Scofield King James Bible is a nice one." I did not understand a word of what she was saying as she placed the Bible on the counter. I sputtered out, "I'll take it!" I just wanted to get out of there. But then doubt set into my mind about trusting that Bible. So I said, "What other types of Bibles do you have?" She said, "We have a New International Bible translated from the original Hebrew and Greek." I was more confused, but I thought I could check one against the other to make sure they said the same things. So I said, "I'll take that one also." I paid for them and exited the Christian bookstore as fast as I could. *Someone might see me in here*, I thought, and I felt very uncomfortable. I walked out of the bookstore and threw both Bibles in the front seat with a sigh of relief. I thought, *I am not going to die. I bought the Bibles and I am safe. I have a feeling of being safe for now, because I have obeyed that voice.* The voice was no longer echoing in my head but the experience is forever etched in my mind like words written on a huge rock of granite.

This point in time was and is the most pivotal moment of my life. I wish I could say everything was just great from that moment on. Believe me, it was not. I was still the same person who was thinking lustful thoughts all day long. Even though I had a supernatural experience with the Lord, I was still a bar owner in Hopedale, Illinois. I began to read the Bible to find out the truth. I would not read the commentary in the Bible because I was looking for God to show me the truth and not the commentator's thoughts. How did I know the truth was in the Bible? The voice told me to buy a Bible. I wasn't looking for any specific religious experience. In fact I was interested in having a good time and letting the chips fall as they came. Before this time in my life if you had tried to tell me about your religion, I would have chewed you up with words. "So you have a corner on God," I would say. "You, of all the people who have ever lived, have all the answers?" I would laugh in your face. "Do you think that God prefers you above anyone else?" I would ask. "Drink, eat, and have fun while you can." If anybody tried to give me the heaven versus hell sermon, I would respond with, "At least I will be with my friends; that's more than I can say for you."

Now I was reading the Bible, of all things, because I had heard the voice and didn't want to die. I must have been programmed to shut out any religious experiences in my life. I did not want anybody to influence how God was going to direct me, so I would ask God all kinds of questions. Then as I read the Bible, God would show me the answers to my questions. I didn't always get an immediate answer when I read the Bible and sometimes I would get my answer from someone who didn't even know they were giving me an answer to a question I had asked God. An individual might say something that would trigger a light of understanding in my head. As I continued reading the Bible in private, people began to find out. People with good intentions came to me and tried to talk me out of what they considered a religious brainwashing or something.

All I knew was that the voice had told me to buy a Bible. If God wanted me to buy a Bible, He must want me to read it. I would be drunk after work late at night sitting in a rocking chair with a bottle of booze in one hand and the Bible in the other hand reading. I was reading and not understanding the Bible, but that voice had said to buy a Bible and I didn't want to die. So I would read on. I was beginning to feel better on the inside, but I didn't know why. Peace would come to me in tough times as I continued reading the Bible. I started reading from the front just like one would read any book. One day I started skipping around and reading wherever the Bible opened. I landed in Proverbs and read a couple of

Scriptures. I understood most of the things in Proverbs and began to read it a lot. So I stumbled through this time in my life motivated by that voice to press onward by reading the Bible. People who knew me the best didn't understand why I was reading the Bible. I was not about to tell them that God had spoken to me that day when I was driving to Peoria for bar supplies.

This situation created multiple problems for me and everyone I loved the most. People began to talk about me behind my back. I knew it. But what was I to do? I felt my only options were to read on or die. So I kept reading the Bible in spite of the changing situation around me. I had built a pretty good business in Hopedale. I had always tried to maintain a good business in the community. Most of the time I was a good businessman, but I made my share of stupid mistakes. Besides that, I had the moral behavior of a male alley cat most of the time.

I believe you can see the conflicting circumstances of life I found myself in. I have never heard the audible voice of God since that day. I say "audible" because I feel like I heard God's voice with my physical ears. The voice was not simply a strong impulse out of my conscience or my mind conjuring something up. Looking back, I realize that the voice was a divine appointment with the All Powerful One who created the heavens and the earth. My whole life has been changed. I've gone from being a person who would rarely read to a person consumed with reading the Bible. Before this moment of time, I looked at the Bible as just another religious book. I wanted nothing to do with religion because religion took advantage of people and caused them to be influenced and controlled for someone else's benefit. I saw people following other religious people blindly as sheep following their masters to a slaughterhouse. I saw no good in organized religion, and I had little to do with any religious groups. I liked most people and wanted to go through life as if it were one big party. I wanted to have all the fun I could, enjoy life, work hard, play hard, and take advantage of every opportunity that came my way.

But now I had heard the voice of God. He had told me to buy a Bible. If the voice had told me to buy any other book, I would have done it. For years I have continued to read the Bible. Since God spoke these words to me, I have been motivated to read the Bible. I carry one with me all of the time, and I always have the Bible near me. I believe anyone who experienced that voice would have obeyed or died. It's really that simple. I have never had the fear of death so strong in my entire life. What choice did I have? I guess one could say it was a no-brainer.

I know one finds this experience hard to believe, but let the facts speak for themselves. My whole world was turned on a dime. Why? What on earth could give a person the passion to read a book he wanted nothing to do with? Now I listen to the Bible on tape driving to work. One may say, "You only thought this happened." Okay, let's look at it from that point of view. Whether I thought it happened or whether it truly happened is only proven by the action taken after the experience. I have had a lot of thoughts. Some I have acted on and some I have not, but none have given me this long-term motivational change of direction. Even if you think I only thought this happened, the end result of my life since the experience has to stand as a testimony of the truth.

I had built a bar and restaurant business based on a home-town cozy environment. Many of my customers were what you would call regulars. They were farmers, construction workers, and factory workers mostly. They had become my friends, and I knew things about almost every one of them. The way I built my business was by listening to what my customers wanted and then supplying the need. I have drunk some type of alcohol with most of them on numerous occasions. But the moment I heard the voice of God, I began to change. The world as I knew it before that afternoon drive to Peoria was not changing. I was! The very business I was proud of building became more and more difficult to run. My values began to change the more I read the Bible. I began to feel like a crab in a bucket. Have you ever heard about catching crabs out of the ocean? When you get your first crab caught, you need to put a lid on the bucket, because the crab will crawl out of the bucket. As soon as you catch your second crab and place him in the bucket, however, you don't need the lid anymore. The reason for this is that as soon as one crab starts to crawl out of the bucket, the other one will reach up and pull him back down in the bucket. So the crabs are constantly watching the other crabs and keeping them in the bucket. As I continued to read the Bible, my desire to keep my bar and restaurant business began to fade. It began to feel like I was in a bucket and all of my customers were fellow crabs trying to keep me in the bucket.

I was changing on the inside. This change was causing a problem with my bar business. As time went on, I hated to tend bar. Before God spoke to me that day, I was as good a bartender as you could find. I loved the excitement that seemed to generate in that environment. The busier I was, the more I liked it. I used to get a kick out of getting a customer to drink another drink. It was a challenge to keep customers in my bar when they knew they had to leave. I would do all sorts of things to keep their interest. But as time went on, I began to want them not to drink. Instead of working to keep them there, I began to want them to quit drinking alcohol.

I bought the bar March 22, 1972, when I was only twenty-two years old and on September 31, 1981, I walked out of the bar and restaurant business in Hopedale forever in obedience to what I believed God was showing me in the Bible. Now I am fifty-six years old, and I believe I am finally fulfilling the purpose God has given me. God has shown me things in the Bible that I am amazed at. Because of this, I am writing this book as an aid for you to understand how and why we are in this present world.

In laying the foundation for the understanding of creation, we need to understand that the Bible is the final authority for all of creation. Any explanation of creation other than what the Bible explains is man's way of guessing how we were created. The Bible is not one man's opinion because more than forty different people have written the sixty-six books or letters that make up the Bible. The Bible has taken thousands of years to complete. The Scriptures have always been considered Holy. The Bible is God's Word to a separated world. Some people have said you cannot trust the Bible because of the age of the Bible. These people say that throughout time people have changed the meanings of the Scriptures. The first of many Dead Sea Scrolls found in 1947 have proven the Bible to be trustworthy. You see, most of these scrolls date back to the time of Jesus. Therefore, one can check the modern-day Scriptures with the newly found old Scriptures. Because they match perfectly, one can trust the words written in the Bible. The Bible means what it says and says what it means. We just need to do what it says in 2 Timothy.

> Study earnestly to present yourself approved to God, a workman that does not need to be ashamed, rightly dividing the Word of Truth. (2 Timothy 2:15, Modern King James Version)

Most of the major religions in the world quote the Bible. Every motivational book written to improve human character uses spiritual laws written in the pages of the Bible. The Bible stands alone in its writings; no other book in this world has had the same amount of time spent on it. The Bible took more years to write than other books last. It doesn't matter how you look at the Bible, it stands head and shoulders above any other book. If you look at the Bible from just its artistic value, there is no match. The historical value of the Bible stands alone as far as books are concerned. Science continually proves the Bible to be true. Any way you approach the Bible, you will find the truth if you have a pure heart and a desire to learn.

I have endeavored to write *Genesis 1-2-3* in a way that anyone would be able to understand it. When I first started to write, I thought the book would be hard to understand for some people. You do not have to read *Genesis 1-2-3* from front to back. You can jump around from chapter to chapter. This book's sole purpose is to be an aid to understanding the Scriptures on creation. Some people may not agree with all of what I have written. This book was not written to create controversy. *Genesis 1-2-3* was written to explain the many questions I and my friends have had about God and creation.

Everyone who has breath in his or her lungs is one of God's creations. How individuals choose to respond to truth makes all the difference in this world and in the world to come. I hope *Genesis 1-2-3* blesses you as much as it blessed me to write it.

God Bless!
Dwight O. Troyer
Hebrew 11:6

Chapter 1

Finding the True Source of All Creation

The creation of earth, as we know it, is something that all of humanity has made continual efforts to understand throughout the ages. People of all walks of life have pursued the answers to the beginning of the earth. The scientific thinkers of this world have formulated different concepts. These new concepts have been given names such as the Big Bang Theory, String Theory, Theory of Natural Selection, and the Theory of Evolution. There are many questions about creation that have gone unanswered, and some questions about creation have been answered over periods of time. Some theories about creation have been accepted as fact or popular belief, only to be proven wrong through the process of time. An example of this is the belief that the earth is flat. People were executed for saying the earth was round and trying to teach their beliefs. Some theories have given birth to new questions. Popular beliefs of the scientific thinkers have changed throughout the ages. Most of the popular concepts on creation have been intertwined with religious beliefs of that corresponding age. Even ways of interpreting the Bible have been changed to fit the popular beliefs of the time. Manuscripts have been written on the different concepts of creation. Great minds have stumbled at

t aspects of creation. In the end there are two basic
ints.

1. Some higher life-form created everything.
2. Everything has been created by chance.

These two basic viewpoints are the foundations used for
all of creational theory. The entire motive to come up with
the perfect creational aspect of life has come from these two
ways of thinking. Individuals have approached life as we
know it and have perfected their beliefs to approach creation
from either one of these viewpoints. To break the concept
down to its simplest form, we must say that the central question regarding the origin of the earth is: Does God exist or
not?

If we believe that God does not exist, we come up with
concepts like the Theory of Evolution this theory believes
that all of the things created have developed through billions
and billions of years of change and development. That all
things have developed from single-cell life-forms. Even
though this theory is highly flawed and leads to many unanswered questions, most people of the age we live in are
taught this theory as fact. If you watch any video on the
Discovery Channel or other educational programming about
reptiles or any other species, you will find that the information will always be presented from an evolutionary point of
view. The concept of evolution has never been proven, but
this concept has birthed many beneficial approaches to the
study of all life-forms. One of the beneficial approaches to
life has caused man to divide species according to common
characteristics. The more we study individual life-forms in
depth, the more we see that evolution has no possibility of
truth. Yet the people who choose to believe in evolution find
it hard to let go of the evolutionary mind-set. They will argue
for the core of their beliefs and show you many reasons to

believe what they say through their own personal convictions. It seems as though evolutionists have been so focused on proving they are right that they have missed all of the evidence throughout the investigation and are unable to see the truth. If these evolutionary believers see something that they cannot explain according to their Theory Of Evolution, like the solid rocky rings of the planet Saturn, they choose to ignore them and stay in the blindness of their own minds. Did you know that 96 percent of United States' citizens believe in some form of a creator, even though the educational system has been teaching evolution as a fact?

Evolution, in biology, complex process by which the characteristics of living organisms change over many generations as traits are passed from one generation to the next. The science of evolution seeks to understand the biological forces that caused ancient organisms to develop into the tremendous and ever-changing variety of life seen on Earth today. It addresses how, over the course of time, various plant and animal species branch off to become entirely new species, and how different species are related through complicated family trees that span millions of years.

Evolution provides an essential framework for studying the ongoing history of life on Earth. A central, and historically controversial, component of evolutionary theory is that all living organisms, from microscopic bacteria to plants, insects, birds, and mammals, share a common ancestor. Species that are closely related share a recent common ancestor, while distantly related species have a common ancestor further in the past. The animal most closely related to humans, for example, is the chimpanzee. The common ancestor of humans and chimpanzees is believed to have lived approximately 6 million to 7 million years ago (*see* Human Evolution). On the other hand, an ancestor common to humans and reptiles lived some 300 million years ago. And the common ancestor to even more distantly related forms lived even further in the past. Evolutionary biologists attempt to determine the history of lineages as they diverge and how differences in characteristics developed over time.

Throughout history, philosophers, religious thinkers, and scientists have attempted to explain the history and variety of life on Earth. During the rise of modern science in Western Europe in the 17th and 18th centuries, a predominant view held that God created every organism on Earth more or less as it now exists. But in that time of burgeoning interest in the study of fossils and natural history, the beginnings of a modern evolutionary theory began to take shape. Early evolutionary theorists proposed that all of life on Earth evolved gradually from simple organisms. Their knowledge of science was incomplete, however, and their theories left too many questions unanswered. *Most prominent scientists of the day remained convinced that the variety of life on Earth could only result from an act of divine creation* [italics added].[1]

It is amazing to me that after all of the in-depth explanation of what defines evolution, the *Microsoft Encarta Encyclopedia 2000* makes the statement highlighted in italic type. The encyclopedia seems to be stating the facts regarding evolution and then slaps you in the face with the fact that most prominent scientists in the 17th and 18th were convinced of a divine creator. Modern Evolutionists are so focused on the created things, they don't see the Creator.

They are not able to think beyond the realm of the flesh. This why the scriptures say...

> These people belong to the world. That's why they speak the thoughts of the world, and the world listens to them. (1John 4:5, God's Word)

This type of thinking hinders the spirit of truth and shows a lack of a deeper perspective of life. Evolutionists focus on the here and now. They find it difficult, if not impossible, to think beyond the things of the flesh. So let us consider this core value question: Does God exist?

No one can answer this question for you personally. Only you have the power to choose which way to believe. Is there a Creator or not? If you choose to believe there is no Creator involved in the creation of the earth, then look at this book as a way of creating more needless information for you, because at the end of your physical life in this world, you will be finished. Please let me tickle your mind with my thoughts on creation.

Let us assume from this point forward that there is a Creator. Let us just say that we believe that some Higher Power has created all things that we see. This Creator has to be something awesome. When we look at the variety of life-forms in this world, it is hard to grasp a firm understanding of this Great Creator. We see the earth and the universe in perfect balance and harmony. We see marvelous plant and animal life. We see wonderful interaction between all living things. We also see birth (new life) everywhere, and we see death (termination) everywhere. Why? Here is a series of questions we can ask ourselves about this Great Creator.

1. Does this Great Creator still exist, or could this Great Creator be separated from us?

2. If this Great Creator was an eternal being that was separated from us, then does this Great Creator care about us?

3. If this Great Creator cares about us, how would this Great Creator express Himself to us since He is separated from us?

4. If this Great Creator were continually expressing Himself to us, would we all understand His expression given our individual complex thought processes and individual choices?

5. How would this Great Creator pick beings to express Himself to?

6. If this Great Creator cared about us all equally, then could this Great Creator pick certain persons with the proper thought processes to communicate His desire for each of us?

7. Could this Great Creator have communicated important information for us all thousands of years ago?

8. If this Great Creator was separated from us and did communicate important information to us, how could He keep it pure?

9. Why does all of humanity have the capability to read and write?

10. How many types of animals can read and write? Why?

11. Could there be a divine purpose for us in reading and writing?

12. Could writing be a way of keeping the divine purpose for all of us pure?

I know the questions above are worded in order to guide an individual to a certain position. We always need to ask ourselves questions, because questions will always open our minds and enlarge the boundaries of our minds to see new ways of looking at things. We can ask ourselves many questions about the Great Creator. The key to finding this Great Creator is to find out where the right answers are.

If we are interested in looking up the definition of a specific word, we can use a dictionary. The dictionary is a great resource to find the correct meaning and spelling of an individual word. It would be a hard task to find the meaning and/or spelling of a word by picking up a daily newspaper and reading it. One might find interesting new pertinent information in the daily paper, but the chances of finding dictionary-type information in the newspaper for a specific word is slim at best. On the other hand if you were looking to find out more about current events, you would not look in the dictionary. For current events a great source would be the daily newspaper.

Therefore, if one is looking for answers to questions about the Great Creator, one has to find the proper research book. The good news is there are many manuscripts and one can read endlessly on all kinds of topics about creation. The bad news is that all of these manuscripts cannot be true. We have all been birthed into this world by a mother, and our mothers have nurtured us through our innocent years. Our mothers are the beginning of where we start our lives. All mothers instill in their children the fundamentals of truth according to what they believe. If a mother was misinformed as a child, she will raise her child with the same misinformation. Even though all people love their mothers, all mothers have the potential to be wrong in their beliefs. It is not that the mother doesn't love us with a whole heart. It is simply a fact that all mothers cannot be right about creation, because it is impossible for all of them to be right with all of the differing viewpoints. So how do we find the truth about creation? In order to find the truth about creation, we first have to separate ourselves from all preconceived ideas. We have to assume our mothers were misinformed. This is hard to do, because the beliefs that were placed in us by our mothers' nurturing are so strong. In order for all of us to see the truth of creation, we have to open our minds to this way of thinking. If you are struggling with this concept, you are most likely one who has been misinformed. Everyone wants to hold on to the principles and concepts of his or her own mother's beliefs.

We first need to find a manuscript that has taken years and years to create. This manuscript has to have letters for direction to the people of this world we live in. It cannot be a single explanation, because if it were a single explanation from one person, this explanation could be narrow-minded, shortsighted, and opinionated. This document we are looking for has to be an in-depth manuscript written and passed down from generation to generation. This manuscript must grow in information and insight. This manuscript needs to have more than one person's narrow viewpoint, but it has to be in total harmony and balance using a variety of people throughout the ages. This one informational book has to contain the understanding of the complexities of our individual lives, and it has to contain an informational understanding of our creation. If there has been a Great Creator who is separated from us for some reason, then this document must contain an in-depth explanation of that separation. This document has to pass the test of time. This document has to be pertinent for this age and has to fit all proven scientific facts. This manuscript must have only one author, God. The more writers that God gets involved in the production of this manuscript, the easier it will be to prove the authenticity of this manuscript. If this manuscript was written in multiple languages on different continents over thousands of years of time without contradictions, this manuscript could not be a narrow-minded misinterpretation of the creation and purpose of earth. This informational manuscript has to have a depth of perception for the purpose of our existence and the direction for that purpose.

If this manuscript reveals a loving, caring Creator, then this manuscript could not have a private interpretation for a select few. It must be an open book for all of humanity to benefit from. This manuscript must be a benefit to the poor as well as to the rich if this Great Creator loves us all equally. This manuscript must have the purpose of the freedom of choice for each of our individual lives as the end result, versus the forced decision of submission to the authority of a certain man or way of thinking.

There is only one manuscript that fills all of the above qualifications. This manuscript is called the Bible. There is no other manuscript with the diversity of background in its origin and harmonies of artful expression of a great, loving Creator. The Bible stands alone as a witness to a separated world. The Bible is a beacon of light to a world separated from a loving and caring heavenly Father. The Bible is a roadmap for an abundant life in this world.

.

Chapter 2

Laying the Foundation of This Study

The term Bible is derived through Latin from the Greek *biblia*, or "books," the diminutive form of *byblos*, the word for "papyrus" or "paper," which was exported from the ancient Phoenician port city of Biblos. By the time of the Middle Ages the books of the Bible were considered a unified entity.[2]

While there are many religions in this world, three of the major ones believe in the book called Genesis. All three look at this book through different eyes. I see this book as the final authority on creation for the Muslim faith, the Jewish faith, and the Christian faith. Even though these faiths differ on many topics, they all agree that the book of Genesis is God's message to humanity, especially about creation. I have purposed in my heart to write this book in such a way that what I have found hidden in the Scriptures will be fully understood and fully explained. My desire is to bring a new breath of the Spirit of God into your mind and body. I am not into giving people information without giving them the ability to check that what I am telling them is the truth. Anybody who teaches a belief, faith, or religion should always back up their beliefs with documentation and true historical facts. Never follow after blind faith. We should always have a target to aim at. We should never do things in our lives only because, "It is the way of my people," "My family has always believed this way," or "My spiritual leader says to do this or that."

Now we are ready to start this in-depth look at chapters 1, 2, and 3 of Genesis. We will first look at Webster's Dictionary for a clear explanation of Genesis.

Genesis means according to Webster's Dictionary:

GEN'ESIS, n. [See Gender.]
1. The first book of the sacred scriptures of the Old Testament, containing the history of the creation, of the apostasy of man, of the deluge, and of the first patriarchs, to the death of Joseph. In the original Hebrew, this book has no title; the present title was prefixed to it by those who translated it into Greek [underline added]

The first three chapters of Genesis are about the history of the creation of the heaven and the earth. These Scriptures of how God created the heaven and the earth are what we are going to focus on. I call these three chapters the ABCs of the creation of this world, as we know it now. I will use these Scriptures as a springboard to launch us into a better understanding of the Bible. The Holy Bible is always true. One needs to rightly divide the truth of God's Word (2 Timothy 2:15). If we need to rightly divide God's Word, we always need to keep in mind that we could wrongly divide God's Word. The Bible I prefer the most is the Modern King James Version for this reason: the majority of time I use this Bible. The King James Version is also easy to use for researching word studies.

In addition we also learn from Webster's Dictionary that Genesis is the name given to this book by those who translated it into Greek. Before it was translated into Greek, it was only written in Hebrew and the Scriptures had no numbering, chapters, verses, or titles. Therefore we need to research the original Hebrew words to study the meanings of these words.

The first verse (Genesis 1:1) written in Hebrew looks like this:

Genesis 1:1

בראשית ברא אלהים את השמים ואת הארץ
הארץ

Hebrew is written from the right side of the paper to the left side of the paper, and one would also read Hebrew from the right side to left side. I cannot read Hebrew, but I can look up the meaning of the Hebrew words using different study guides. One of the most recognized study guides is *Strong's Exhaustive Concordance*. I find it the most helpful to use. I will use the *Strong's Exhaustive Concordance* the most in the first few chapters of this book to establish a more indepth understanding of the meanings of the original Hebrew words. One has to build a strong foundation in definitions of words to proceed with the construction of an informative book. As we advance in this study, I will use additional cross-references of the Scriptures to bring more clarity.

Hebrew words written with the modern day alphabet system look like this:

tyvarb arb Myhla ta Mymvh taw .Crah
(Genesis 1:1)

We know this verse in King James English as:

In the beginning God created the heavens and the earth. (Genesis 1:1, King James Version)

I cannot read Hebrew, and it is difficult for me to sound out the Hebrew words using the modern alphabet. But just as I looked up the meaning of the word *Genesis* in the *Webster's Dictionary*, I can look up the individual Hebrew words using *Strong's Exhaustive Concordance*. Years ago this would have been harder for me to do, but with the help of a computer, this research has been made faster and easier.

To summarize we can see that the original Scriptures were written in Hebrew, translated into Greek, and then translated into other languages. With the help of *Strong's Exhaustive Concordance*, we can find the original Hebrew word for each English word and get a better understanding of that word. In addition to this, the meanings of our words are constantly changing.

This is how it works:

In the beginning[7225] God[430] created[1254] [(853)] the heaven[8064] and the earth.[776] (Genesis 1:1 King James Version w/ Strong's Numbers)

In the above verse there are numbers behind some of the words. Each Hebrew word is assigned one number. These numbers are quick reference numbers that help us find the meaning in the English language of the Hebrew word used. These numbers are found in *Strong's Exhaustive Concordance*. Find a specific word in *Strong's Exhaustive Concordance* in alphabetical order. Then find the chapter and verse for that specific word. You can research the word, find the number for the Hebrew word, and expand your understanding of that word. *Strong's Exhaustive Concordance* also has a Greek section for the New Testament. It uses a numbering system also. This wording and numbering has been simplified by Rick Meyer's e-sword software at e-sword.com.

Example: In the beginning[7225]

> 7225 - Hebrew
> 7225 re'shiyth ray-sheeth'
> from the same as 7218; the first, in place, time, order or rank (specifically, a firstfruit): — beginning, chief (-est), first(-fruits, part, time), principal thing. [3]

Notice that this definition gives more information about the grouping of the words *in the beginning* because our English words are not as complex as the Hebrew words. This single word in Hebrew takes a grouping of English words to explain what it means. "In the beginning" means:

1. The first in place, time, order, or rank.
2. The first fruit, first part, or first time.
3. The principal thing or the chief(-est).
4. The beginning.

Now let us take these tools and start an in-depth study of Genesis. We will start with the word *days*. This word *days* is crucial to understanding Genesis 1 and 2. This word *days* is used over and over in the first chapter and follows into the first half of the second chapter. Let's look at the word *days*, find its number, and look at the definition of that number using *Strong's Exhaustive Concordance*.

And God called the light Day [3117], and the darkness he called Night. And the evening and the morning were the first day [3117]. (Genesis 1:5, king James Version w/two Strong's Numbers)

3117 - Hebrew
yome

From an unused root meaning to *be hot*; a *day* (as the *warm* hours), whether literally (from sunrise to sunset, or from one sunset to the next), or figuratively (a space of time defined by an associated term), (often used adverbially): - age, + always, + chronicles, continually (-ance), daily, ([birth-], each, to) day, (now a, two) days (agone), + elder, X end, + evening, + (for) ever (-lasting, -more), X full, life, as (so) long as (. . . live), (even) now, + old, + outlived, + perpetually, presently, + remaineth, X required, season, X since, space, then, (process of) time, + as at other times, + in trouble, weather, (as) when, (a, the, within a) while (that), X whole (+ age), (full) year (-ly), + younger.[4]

Notice by this definition we see that the word *day* can mean:

1) A hot time.
2) Sunup to sunset.
3) Sunset to sunset.
4) A space of time (large or small).

Just to make myself clear, this word has more meanings then I have numbered above, but these four meanings are sufficient to cover all of the meanings that are connected with the first three chapters of Genesis.

The creation of the heavens and of the earth are divided into what the Bible says are days.

And God called the light, Day. And He called the darkness, Night. And the evening and the morning were <u>the first day</u>. (Genesis 1:5, Modern King James Version, underline added)

And God called the expanse, Heavens. And the evening and the morning were <u>the second day</u>. (Genesis 1:8, Modern King James Version, underline added)

And the evening and the morning were <u>the third day</u>. (Genesis 1:13, Modern King James Version, underline added)

And the evening and the morning were <u>the fourth day</u>. (Genesis 1:19, Modern King James Version, underline added)

And the evening and the morning were <u>the fifth day</u>. (Genesis 1:23, Modern King James Version, underline added)

And God saw everything that He had made, and behold, it was very good. And the evening and the morning were <u>the sixth day</u>. (Genesis 1:31, Modern King James Version, underline added)

And on <u>the seventh day</u> God ended His work which He had made. And He rested on the seventh day from all His work which He had made. (Genesis 2:2, Modern King James Version, underline added)

We can look at each one of these days in any four of these meanings; a hot time, a twenty-four hour period of time, sunup until sundown, or a space of time (large or small). Please note the words *evening and morning were the ___ day*. *Evening* means "sundown" and *morning* means "sunrise." If the Scriptures were stating a twenty-four hour period of time for the meaning of the word *day*, the inspired writer would not have described the nighttime as "the ___ day." The writer would have stated, "Morning and evening were the ____ day" or "sunset to sunset was the ____ day." The description of each day indicates that God created all these things in the nighttime as far as sunrise and sunset are concerned.

Daylight

(Morning)Sunrise   Sundown(Evening)

Nighttime

In the evening time (sundown), we are going into a period of darkness. This is the starting part of this darkness and as we see things today the sunrise brings the new light of each day. In our finite minds we look at things from a black and white type of mind set. Please keep in mind the sun, moon, planets, and stars were made the fourth day, therefore this is not expressing a twenty-four hour cycle. In order to find a more precise meaning of the word *day* that is being conveyed in each instance, we can use these clues to help us:

❖ Look in front of the particular topic.
❖ Look at the end of the particular topic.
❖ Look for a reflective topic within the topic.

For example, in this case we find the meaning of the word *days* that is being expressed by looking right after the last day expressed.

And on the seventh day God ended His work which He had made. And He rested on the seventh day from all His work which He had made. And God blessed the seventh day and sanctified it, because in it He had rested from all His work which God created to make. <u>These are the generations of the heavens and of the earth when they were created</u>. (Genesis 2:2–4, Modern King James Version, underline added)

One needs to understand that when the Bible was written, it did not have chapters and verses. Names of the books were applied to the manuscripts, and they were broken down into chapters and verses to have a point of reference for teaching and learning. Therefore, verses in the next chapter may be an extension of the preceding chapter.

For example:

These *are* the generations of the heavens and of the earth when they were created. (Genesis 2:4, Modern King James Version)

Let us look at the first word of this verse. What is the word *these* referring to? The word *these* has to be referring to "days." So I believe we could paraphrase this verse as follows for explanation purposes.

These [days] are the generations of the heavens and of the earth when they were created. (Genesis 2:4, author's paraphrase)

Notice also the word *generations*. The *s* at the end of *generation* means "more than one." So we could say each day is one generation.

Strong's Exhaustive Concordance gives the definition of *generations* as:

8435 - Hebrew
8435 towldah to-led-aw'

or toldah to-led-aw'; from 3205; (plural only) descent, i.e. family; (figuratively) history:—birth, generations. [5]

To amplify the meaning of this verse we could paraphrase the Word of God like this:

Each one of these seven days represents a generation of the heavens and of the earth when they were created. (Genesis 2:4, author's paraphrase)

This verse tells about the creation of the heaven and the earth. This verse also explains which definition of the word *days* is expressed. The word *day* being used in all of the previous verses is expressing the history or generations of creation not a twenty-four hour period of time. The Word of God implies by this wording that it was a process over a dispensation or a space in a dimension. This realm of creation was in eternity and each generation was a portion of measurement in that realm.

Young's Literal Translation says:

These *are* births of the heavens and of the earth in their being prepared. (Genesis 2:4) [6]

Young's Literal Translation calls the creation period "births" and anyone who has had children knows there is a process that takes place in a birth. One has to have conception and the development of the baby in the womb before one nears the final stage of delivery. There is heavy, hurtful labor that takes place with spasms of pain between a steady ache during the delivery alone, not to mention the morning sickness, the kicking, the rolling, and all the punching and pulling that goes on in the process. Even though I could never give birth personally, I have five children, and I have been present during three of their births. Giving birth is work!

God created the heaven and the earth in what was called "generations." These dispensations of time were said to be finished in Genesis 2:1–2. Not only that, but the whole host of them.

> Thus the heavens and the earth were finished[3615], and all the host of them. And on the seventh day God ended[3615] his work which he had made; and he rested on the seventh day from all his work which he had made. (Genesis 2:1–2, King James Version w/two Strong's Numbers)

When one looks at the two words *finished* and *ended* in Genesis 2:1–2, one will notice by the number following these words that they both mean the same thing and are the exact same Hebrew word used in both verses. One can see that the same word is used because of the number used (3615) to designate which Hebrew word was used in the original Scriptures. The definition of that word according to *Strong's Exhaustive Concordance* is:

> 3615 kalah kaw-law'
> a primitive root; to end, whether intransitive (to cease, be finished, perish) or transitively (to complete, prepare, consume):—accomplish, cease, consume (away), determine, destroy (utterly), be (when . . . were) done, (be an) end (of), expire, (cause to) fail, faint, finish, fulfil, X fully, X have, leave (off), long, bring to pass, wholly reap, make clean riddance, spend, quite take away, waste. [7]

So we could say that God created the heavens and the earth, and they were completed. He had totally finished all of

39

His work, the Bible says, and He was resting in the seventh day (generation). Please keep in mind that this realm of creation is what I call an eternal realm. Everything according to this verse looks good. Except for one phrase stuck in between the word *finished* and *ended*. This phrase is:

... the host[6635] of them. (Genesis 2:1, King James Version, w/one Strong's Number)

These four English words came from this one Hebrew word. *Strong's Exhaustive Concordance* gives the definition of this word as:

6635 - Hebrew
tsaˆbaˆ' tsebaˆ'aˆh
tsaw-baw', tseb-aw-aw'
From H6633; a mass of persons (or figurative things), especially regularly organized for war (an army); by implication a campaign, literally or figuratively (specifically hardship, worship): - appointed time, (+) army, (+) battle, company, host, service, soldiers, waiting upon, war (-fare).[8]

Apparently there was a war or battle going on in the heaven and earth that God had just created. If there was not a battle going on, there was at least a mass of things organized for war implicating a campaign of hardship waiting for war. I also believe there was a host of things ready to worship. God did not go to war. Instead of going to war, God rested! So why did He rest? Because He always has everything under control, and because He is a God of faith who called those things that be not as though they are. Romans 4:17 in the International Standard Version explains God's ability to create using faith in this manner.

Who gives life to the dead and calls into existence things that don't even exist. (Romans 4:17,
International Standard Version)[9]

Let us look a little deeper into what God rested from. In
order to find out a little more about the Scriptures in Genesis,
let us look at the first day (generation). We will go through
each day later, but we need to establish some foundational
understanding. Genesis chapter one is the beginning part.
You remember the very first word we investigated was the
word *beginning*.

Beginning means:

1. The first in place, time, order, or rank.
2. The first fruit, first part, or first time.
3. The principal thing or the chief.
4. The beginning.

This beginning time is the starting place for God's creation
of the heaven and the earth. It is not the starting time of God,
because God always has been. He is an eternal being; He has
no beginning or end. The Scriptures tell us what His character is and who He is. Therefore this beginning time is the
beginning of the creation of heaven and earth. Scriptures are
multifaceted, meaning there are different layers of meaning
within the Scriptures. We can look at the surface and be
blessed, but as we grow, we look at the same Scriptures and
the Holy Spirit shows us deeper things. So let us look at
the first day (generation) as written in Modern King James
Version.

In the beginning God created the heavens and the
earth. And the earth was without form and empty.
And darkness *was* on the face of the deep. And the
Spirit of God moved on the face of the waters. And

God said, Let there be light. And there was light. And God saw the light that *it was* good. And God divided between the light and the darkness. And God called the light, Day. And He called the darkness, Night. And the evening and the morning were the first day. (Genesis 1:1–5, Modern King James Version)

Looking at the Scriptures that pertain to the first day (generation), we can see how God began the creation of the heavens and the earth. In the first day (generation), we do not see the why. Now we are not going to look at the why or the how, but we will focus in on the what. What did God do in this day to begin the creation of the heaven and the earth? God created light and divided between light and darkness. Let us look at light and darkness. I had never done a word study on the creation of light and darkness until I started writing this book.

And God saw the light[216], that it was good[2896]. (Genesis 1:4, King James Version w/two Strong's Numbers)

We see from the previous verse that God created the light and this verse goes on to explain the light.

1. God saw the light.
2. God acknowledged the light to be good.

Looking again at *Strong's Exhaustive Concordance*, we see the meaning of these two words from the original Hebrew language:

(light[216])
216 'owr ore

from 215; illumination or (concrete) luminary (in every sense, including lightning, happiness, etc.):— bright, clear, + day, light(-ning), morning, sun. [10]

Light means all aspects of light. Light also includes happiness which is an emotion.

(good[2896])
2896 towb tobe
from 2895; good (as an adjective) in the widest sense; used likewise as a noun, both in the masculine and the feminine, the singular and the plural (good, a good or good thing, a good man or woman; the good, goods or good things, good men or women), also as an adverb (well):—beautiful, best, better, bountiful, cheerful, at ease, X fair (word), (be in) favour, fine, glad, good (deed, -lier, -liest, -ly, -ness, -s), graciously, joyful, kindly, kindness, liketh (best), loving, merry, X most, pleasant, + pleaseth, pleasure, precious, prosperity, ready, sweet, wealth, welfare, (be) well ([-favoured]). [11]

Good has no gender and is beautiful, best, better, bountiful, cheerful, at ease, favor, fine, glad, graciously, joyful, kindly, kindness, loving, merry, pleasure, precious, sweet, wealth, welfare, and prosperity.

So I guess we could say light is all right (very fine). We also need to investigate the second half of this same verse using Strong's Hebrew and Greek Dictionaries.

And God divided[914, 996] the light from the darkness[2822]. (Genesis 1:4, King James Version w/three Strong's Numbers)

(divided[914])
914 badal baw-dal'
a primitive root; to divide (in variation senses literally or figuratively, separate, distinguish, differ,
select, etc.):—(make, put) difference, divide
(asunder), (make) separate (self, -ation), sever (out),
X utterly.[12]

Divide means to distinguish, sever, differentiate,
separate.

(darkness[2822])
2822 choshek kho-shek'
from 2821; the dark; hence (literally) darkness;
figuratively, misery, destruction, death, ignorance,
sorrow, wickedness:—dark(-ness), night, obscurity.
[13]

This Hebrew word for *darkness* does not just mean
"night" or "absence of light." This Hebrew word also means
misery, destruction, death, ignorance, sorrow, wickedness,
obscurity.
Let us now look at the same verse in light of the deeper
Hebrew meanings for each word.

And God saw the [happy, bright, clear, sunrise] light
that it was [beautiful, best, better, bountiful, cheerful,
at ease, favor, fine, glad, graciously, joyful, kindly,
kindness, loving, merry, pleasure, precious, sweet,
wealth, prosperous] good. And God [distinguished,
severed, differentiated, separated] divided between
the [happy, bright, clear, sun rise] light and the
[misery, destruction, death, ignorance, sorrow, wickedness, obscurity] darkness. (Genesis 1:4, author's
additions)

In the first day (generation) of the beginning part of the creation of heaven and earth, it looks like there is a conflict happening. Not that it was a problem with God, because God created all things for His good pleasure. God always acts in response to any circumstance with faith. God is a faith-filled, working God. Let us look at what we know about Genesis this far.

1. The Book of Genesis was written in Hebrew first.
2. It received the name "Genesis" from the Greek translators.
3. The Bible did not have book titles (names), chapters, or verse numbers. These were added to help in teaching and studying.
4. Every word in the Old Testament King James Version can be traced to the original Hebrew word with the use of a *Strong's Bible Dictionary.*
   A. Uses a numbering system for the Hebrew words.
   B. The words in English are listed in alphabetical order.
   C. Each use of the referenced word in the Bible is listed by chapter and verse.

5. The Hebrew word for *days* means:
   A. A hot time.
   B. Sunup to sundown.
   C. Twenty-four hour period of time.
   D. A period of time (large or small).

6. God moved in faith.
   A. Through the darkness (evening or sundown).
   B. Toward the morning (sunup).
   7. Each one of the seven days of creation represents one generation.

8. Together they are the finished product of the creation of heaven and earth.

9. The seventh day was the final generation of the creation of heaven and earth.
    A. There was a host prepared for war.
    B. There was a host prepared for worship.
    C. God rested!

10. First day (generation) God created the light.
    A. *Light* is not just all elements of light but happy.

11. Signified the light as being good.
    A. *Good* means all aspects of an abundant life.

12. Separated the darkness from the light.
    A. *Darkness* means all aspects of a miserable life.

Chapter 3

The Six Creative Days of the Heaven and Earth

We have established that the creation periods God calls "days" in Genesis 1 and 2 were generations. We also have acknowledged that in the first day there was a separation of light and darkness. We also saw that in the beginning of the creation of heaven and earth, there were many different beings that were already present with God. Apparently there was a war or battle going on with God while He created heaven and earth. If there was not a battle going on, there was at least a group of things or beings organized for war indicating a campaign of hardship waiting for war. We also saw that God created the heaven and earth from sundown to sunup, indicating that He constructed the heavens and the earth in the presence of darkness. Let us also note that the earth, sun, moon, and stars were not made until the fourth creation period, but God still called the evening and morning the first day (generation). So in the first day (generation), we can see that the sun, moon, and stars had not been created. There was no dry land (earth). Let us look at Genesis 1.

In the beginning God created the heavens and the earth. And the earth was without form and empty.

And darkness was on the face of the deep. And the Spirit of God moved on the face of the waters. And God said, Let there be light. And there was light. And God saw the light that it was good. And God divided between the light and the darkness. And God called the light, Day. And He called the darkness, Night. And the evening and the morning were the first day. (Genesis 1:1–5, Modern King James Version)

Genesis 1: 1 is the beginning Scripture of the Bible. This verse is the thesis statement of what God is doing in the seven creation periods. Each creation period is a generation that the interpreters of the Bible call "days."

In the beginning God created the heavens and the earth. (Genesis 1:1, King James Version)

Notice that heaven and earth have not yet been created in the first generation. The creation of heaven and earth takes a process of time over seven different individual generations. What we see in verse two of this same chapter is a description of the moment God began creation. We need always to keep in mind that the seven generations were not just a creation time for the earth; the entire heavenly realm was created also during this time. The Scriptures do not just say God created the earth. The Scriptures also say God created the heavens during this seven-day creational period.

And the earth was without form and empty. And darkness was on the face of the deep. And the Spirit of God moved on the face of the waters. (Genesis 1:2, Modern King James Version)

Genesis 1:2 said the earth was "without form and empty." "Without form and empty" means there was nothing, because the earth was not made yet. It is hard for us to understand creation because we need to make something from something. What this verse is saying is that there was nothing. The planets and stars did not exist. This verse says three things:

1. The earth did not exist.
2. Darkness was over the water.
3. The Spirit of God was moving over the waters.

I love this story that Pastor Olsten told one evening on his TV program. He told the story in such a way that it brought light to the truth in a funny way. Here is the story as I remember what he said about a scientist and God talking about creating things.

The scientist said, "I can create man or any animal without any problem."

God said, "You can?"

The scientist said, "It would be no problem to produce a living product."

God said, "Do you really think it would be that simple for you?"

The scientist said, "We now have all the gene codes and can create anything."

God said, "Really? Why don't you show Me this?"

The scientist said, "First I'll take this dirt and then . . ."

His voice trailed off because God said, "That's my dirt; make your own dirt!"

We see in this first generation that water was present with God. I believe this is why all of the scientists say that all things evolved out of water or came out of water. If we look at our bodies, we are mostly water. What we eat has nutrition in it, but most of what we consume is water. We have to continually replenish water back into our system. We can live for days without food if it is necessary, but we need to have a constant supply of water. All living things become dry and shrivel up without water. Have you ever seen a body that has been cremated? The body just becomes a lump of dirt. The reason this happens is that all of the water is burned out of the body with intense heat. As the moisture in the body is removed, the body begins to dry. When the fire has expelled the water, the body will begin to burn. Fire breaks the body down quickly to its original components. What you have left is a container of earth.

> Water is the major constituent of living matter. From 50 to 90 percent of the weight of living organisms is water. Protoplasm, the basic material of living cells, consists of a solution in water of fats, carbohydrates, proteins, salts, and similar chemicals. Water acts as a solvent, transporting, combining, and chemically breaking down these substances. Blood in animals and sap in plants consist largely of water and serve to transport food and remove waste material. Water also plays a key role in the metabolic breakdown of such essential molecules as proteins and carbohydrates. This process, called hydrolysis, goes on continually in living cells.[14]

We see that water is the natural resource of life in this world; we see that it is the solution to carry out God's purpose for all of His earthly creations. We see that God had the water before any earth was formed. God's Word says the water was before the dirt; man says by evolution all things evolved out of the dirt by some chance. It was not until the third generation of creation that any form of dirt was made.

The only other thing that was present with God in the beginning was darkness. So what we have is the Spirit of God moving over the water in the presence of darkness. That was all there was described in the beginning of the creation of heaven and earth. Could there have been more? It is possible there were other things, but if there were other things, they are obviously not pertinent to us now in a direct sense. The first day (generation) of heaven and earth is about to begin. The stage is set! The Spirit of God is moving! Darkness is present everywhere! And there is water!

> And God said, Let there be light. And there was light. And God saw the light that it was good. And God divided between the light and the darkness. And God called the light, Day. And He called the darkness, Night. And the evening and the morning were the first day. (Genesis 1:3–5, Modern King James Version)

The first thing that happened was God spoke! When God speaks, things happen! Not just anything happens, but what God says happens. Let us look at what He said:

> And God said, Let there be light. And there was light. (Genesis 1:3, Modern King James Version)

I once heard Kenneth Copeland say while I was watching him on his Television program, "God did not say, 'Let there be light and there was light.' What God really said was, 'Light be, light was!'"

Copeland went on and said, "The interpreters of the Bible have added all of the flowery descriptions, such as 'let there be light.'" [15]

I agree with him. The Bible should say:

And God said, Light be and light was. (Genesis 1:3, author's paraphrase)

This first day (generation) appears to lack a lot of content. There is much more written about the other days of creation. Because of this, the other days appear to be greater accomplishments. I believe each day was equal in value and importance to creating the heavens and the earth.

I once took a tour of a gold mine called the Molly Kathleen Mine in Cripple Creek, Colorado. The tour guide dropped us down the shaft of this mine about five hundred feet and turned off the lights. Talk about dark! You could not see anything. It was so quiet. There were about twelve people on the tour. You could not even hear them breathe. I will always remember the sound of a drip of water in the pitch-black stillness. Then the tour guide said, "Look up!" There, far above us about the size of a golf ball, was light shining into the shaft. He then turned the light on and continued the tour. What an experience!

What we have to understand is that there was nothing but darkness over water with the Holy Spirit in motion, and God said, "Light be!" What a great God of faith we serve. God spoke light into the visual realm; He saw the light and said it was good.

And God saw the light that it was good. (Genesis 1:4)

Light is a form of energy visible to the human eye that is radiated by moving charged particles. Light from the sun provides the energy needed for plant growth. Plants convert the energy in sunlight into storable chemical form through a process called photosynthesis. Petroleum, coal, and natural gas are the remains of plants and the energy these fuels release when they burn is the chemical energy converted from sunlight. When animals digest the plants and animals they eat, they also release energy stored by photosynthesis.

Scientists have learned through experimentation that light behaves like a particle at times and like a wave at other times. The particle like features are called photons. Photons are different from particles of matter in that they have no mass and always move at the constant speed of 300,000 km/sec (186,000 mi/sec) when they are in a vacuum. When light diffracts, or bends slightly as it passes around a corner, it shows wavelike behavior. The waves associated with light are called electromagnetic waves because they consist of changing electric and magnetic fields.[16]

Please note that the sun is not created until the fourth creation period. Let us look at what else God did in the first creation period of the creation of the heavens and earth.

> And God saw the light that it was good. And God divided between the light and the darkness. And God called the light, Day. And He called the darkness, Night. (Genesis 1:4-5, Modern King James Version)

God divided between the light and darkness and gave them the names *day* and *night*. If you have further questions about the light and darkness, you could revisit Chapter two of this book.

> And God called the light, Day. And He called the darkness, Night. <u>And the evening and the morning were the first day.</u> (Genesis 1:5, Modern King James Version, underline added)

One more thing I would like to revisit from the first chapter. This is "the evening and morning was the first day." As I illustrated, evening (sunset) to morning (sunup) was the first day (generation). This is very interesting because the sun, moon, planets, and stars had not been created. At this point in time, according to the Scriptures, the foundation of all the creation of heaven and earth was laid. The foundation God laid included light and water.

These two substances are with God in the beginning of the creation of heaven and earth. All of the things that we now see need these two substances to sustain life. This is the beginning of a process the scientists call *photosynthesis*, a necessary function placed in this world by God. We will look at photosynthesis in a little more depth later, but now we will look at the second day (generation) of the creation of heaven and earth. This second creation period is another foundational function necessary to create a balanced environment for all of God's creations.

> And God said, Let there be an expanse in the middle of the waters, and let it divide the waters from the waters. And God made the expanse, and divided the waters which were under the expanse from the waters which were above the expanse; and it was so. And God called the expanse, Heavens. And the evening and the morning were the second day. (Genesis 1:6–8, Modern King James Version)

The first thing that happened is God spoke. I said before, when God speaks, what He says happens! The Modern King James Version says:

> And God said, Let there be an <u>expanse</u> in the middle of the waters. (Genesis 1:6, Modern King James Version, underline added)

Webster's Dictionary says...

EXPANSE, n. expans'. [L. expansum.] A spreading; extend; a wide extent of space or body; as the expanse of heaven [underline added].

So the way we could say what God said in easy-to-understand terms is:

And God said, Let there be a space in the middle of the waters. (Genesis 1:6, Modern King James Version, underline added)

This space that God has created to separate the water He names heaven. Let us look at what is created now. In day two we see these things created so far in the building processes of creating heaven and earth:

1. Water.
2. Light.
3. Space called heaven.

In day two we see these things separated:

1. Light separated from darkness.
2. Water is separated by a space.

Light is separated from darkness and there are two bodies of water separated by a space that God calls heaven. These two bodies of water would be in a flat, stretched out linear form with a space God named heaven separating them.

We are now ready for the third action God took in the formation of the creation of heaven and earth. We begin to see how God is going to use light and water as primary substances for all living things.

And God said, Let the waters under the heavens be gathered together to one place, and let the dry land appear; and it was so. And God called the dry land, Earth. And He called the gathering together of the waters, Seas. And God saw that it was good. (Genesis 1:9–10, Modern King James Version)

The heavens and earth are beginning to take form; we can begin to see what our God is doing. In this third day, the earth is formed. Let us look at some illustrations of the water and heavens.

WATER

Space (Heaven)

WATER

In the second day we see two bodies of water separated by a space. In the third day we see that God said, "Let all of the waters be gathered together under heaven" (Genesis 1:9). God caused all of the water under the space to be gathered together. The form that the water would have to take for the best possible compaction would be like a ball. This water was most likely folded together from the outer edges, causing the water above the space to surround the gathered-together body of water like a huge water sphere.

The above picture is an illustration of what God spoke in the first part of the third generation of the creation of the heaven and the earth. The dark areas represent the water. The white area between the two bodies of water is a space God called heaven. When God put all the water together under heaven, He created a ball of water separated by a space (heaven). This picture is a two dimensional picture of what I am trying to portray. The outer sphere of water is not like the rings of Saturn but it completely surrounds the ball of water like a terrarium. This outer sphere of water totally surrounds the space and the smaller ball of water. This picture is a cross section of what it would look like, if you cut the sphere, space, and ball of water in half.

We begin to see a form beginning to take shape. Then God said, "Let the dry land appear." So in this ball of water under the sphere of water, God placed dry land. We see that God has spoken everything into existence to this point. Now we see the earth beginning to take form.

In summary of what God has made, one now can see the beginning phases of the formation of earth. Please keep in mind this sphere of water is still around the earth above the space called heaven. Some Christian scientists believe it was frozen and somewhat clear like a window with a fog of moisture on it on an arctic day. The remnant of this ring of water is the ozone layer far above the earth's surface. These scientists believe an asteroid that brought the flood of Noah broke this ring of water. The Scripture that mentions this is in Genesis 7:11. Please realize that all of the other planets, stars, and moons have not been created at this time. Only the dirt of the earth has been created.

As we look at this third day, we see that God created a huge ball of water surrounded by a space with another layer of water above the space, most likely frozen. When God spoke for the dry land to come forth out of the water, the way in which it happened most likely was through volcanic action. Please notice that the water was present before any dry land. Therefore, condensation would occur in an enormous way letting off steam vapors like huge clouds of fog rising off of the surface.

> The earliest atmosphere must have consisted of volcanic emanations alone. Gases that erupt from volcanoes today, however, are mostly a mixture of water vapor, carbon dioxide, sulfur dioxide, and nitrogen, with almost no oxygen. If this is the same mixture that existed in the early atmosphere, then various processes would have had to operate to produce the mixture we have today. One of these processes was condensation. As it cooled, much of the volcanic water vapor condensed to fill the earliest oceans. Chemical reactions would also have occurred. Some carbon dioxide would have reacted with the rocks of the earth's crust to form carbonate minerals, and some would have become dissolved in the new oceans. Later, as primitive life capable of photosynthesis evolved in the oceans, new marine organisms began producing oxygen. Almost all the free oxygen in the air today is believed to have formed by photosynthetic combination of carbon dioxide with water.[17]

In the third day God also created plant life. When God created plant life, He began the production of oxygen, which is a necessary gas for all land-dwelling animals. Every plant is necessary to the balance of God's creations through photosynthesis. In the process of photosynthesis, carbon dioxide is converted to oxygen.

> And God said, Let the earth bring forth tender sprouts (the herb seeding seed and the fruit tree producing fruit after its kind, whose seed is in itself) upon the earth; and it was so. And the earth brought forth tender sprouts, the herb yielding seed after its kind, and the tree producing fruit after its kind, whose seed was in itself. And God saw that it was good. (Genesis 1:11–12, Modern King James Version)

So in the same generation that God created the dry land, God also created all of the plant life. When He created plant life, He also gave it the ability to reproduce itself. The Scriptures say He placed the seed of reproduction in each plant. Each one of these seeds will only produce after its own kind. What God is saying here is that you cannot plant corn and expect an apple tree. It is not going to happen! If you plant corn, you are going to get corn. Every plant will reproduce after its own kind of plant.

> Photosynthesis is a process by which green plants and certain other organisms use the energy of light to convert carbon dioxide and water into the simple sugar glucose. In so doing, photosynthesis provides the basic energy source for virtually all organisms. An extremely important byproduct of photosynthesis is oxygen, on which most organisms depend.
> Photosynthesis occurs in green plants, seaweeds, algae, and certain bacteria. These organisms are veritable sugar factories, producing millions of new glucose molecules per second. Plants use much of

this glucose, a carbohydrate, as an energy source to build leaves, flowers, fruits, and seeds. They also convert glucose to cellulose, the structural material used in their cell walls. Most plants produce more glucose than they use, however, and they store it in the form of starch and other carbohydrates in roots, stems, and leaves. The plants can then draw on these reserves for extra energy or building materials. Each year, photosynthesizing organisms produce about 170 billion metric tons of extra carbohydrates, about 30 metric tons for every person on earth.

Photosynthesis has far-reaching implications. Like plants, humans and other animals depend on glucose as an energy source, but they are unable to produce it on their own and must rely ultimately on the glucose produced by plants. Moreover, the oxygen humans and animals breath is the oxygen released during photosynthesis. Humans are also dependent on products of photosynthesis, known as fossil fuels, for supplying most of our modern industrial energy. These fossil fuels, including natural gas, coal, and petroleum, are composed of a complex mix of hydrocarbons, the remains of organisms that relied on photosynthesis. Thus, virtually all life on earth, directly or indirectly, depends on photosynthesis as a source of food, energy, and oxygen, making it one of the most important biochemical processes known.[18]

And every plant of the field before it was in the earth, and every herb of the field before it grew: for the LORD God had not caused it to rain on the earth, and there was not a man to till the ground. But there went up a mist from the earth, and watered the whole face of the ground. (Genesis 2:5–6, Modern King James Version)

Genesis 2:5–6 gives us a deeper explanation of what the earth was like in its creative stage. There was no rain. A mist (fog or vapor) from the ground watered all of the earth. Notice man was not created yet. The plants grew much like plants in a terrarium grow. Remember that there was a sphere of frozen water surrounding the earth, just like a huge glass globe surrounding and enclosing a terrarium. These plants were also creating oxygen through the process of photosynthesis.

In summary God:

1. Brought the water together under heaven.
2. Caused dry land to appear out of the water.
3. Caused plants to grow out of the land.

During the fourth creative period of the creation of heaven and earth according to the Modern King James Version, God said:

And God said, Let there be lights in the expanse of the heavens to divide between the day and the night. And let them be for signs, and for seasons, and for days and years. And let them be for lights in the expanse of the heavens to give light upon the earth. And it was so. And God made two great lights: the greater light to rule the day and the smaller light to rule the night, and the stars also. And God set them in the expanse of the heavens to give light upon the earth, and to rule over the day and over the night; and to divide between the light and the darkness. And God saw that it was good. And the evening and the morning were the fourth day. (Genesis 1:14–19, Modern King James Version)

So in the fourth day (generation) of the creation of the heavens and earth, God created the sun, moon, planets, and stars. All of them were created for signs, for seasons, for days, and years, according to what the Scripture says in Genesis 1:14.

This expanse of the heavens is above the outer circle of water. So what we now have is a mass of water pulled together into a ball. Then there is a huge space called heaven, which happens to be our atmosphere. Above this atmosphere, there is another body of water most likely frozen. Beyond this outer layer of water is a larger space called heaven also. In this second space God places all of the suns, moons, planets, and stars in the fourth day. Therefore we have a first heaven (atmosphere) and we have a second heaven (outer space).

Something that is of interest is that after the fourth day is complete, the earth now has a sun. At the completion of this day, there is now a twenty-four hour day. This means that from this fourth day forward, one can see a sunup (morning) and a sundown (evening). From the beginning of the fifth day forward, one could say evening to morning and mean sundown to sunup. Before this day, the sun, moon, and stars did not exist. But God has chosen to use in every creation day the expression "evening and morning were the _____ day."

And the evening and the morning were the first day.
(Genesis 1:5, Modern King James Version)
And the evening and the morning were the second day. (Genesis 1:8, Modern King James Version)
And the evening and the morning were the third day.
(Genesis 1:13, Modern King James Version)

And the evening and the morning were the fourth day.
(Genesis 1:19, Modern King James Version)
And the evening and the morning were the fifth day.
(Genesis 1:23, Modern King James Version)
And the evening and the morning were the sixth day.
(Genesis 1:31, Modern King James Version)

As I said before, in the evening time (sundown), we are going into a period of darkness. This is the starting part of this darkness. I believe this period from evening to morning is a dark time when all things that were made, were made. During this time, our God who is full of faith moved by faith even though it looked dark. It looked like it was not going to work. It looked impossible. But God moved forward not looking at the circumstances around Him and persevered through the dark times. The situations did not appear to be working in the midnight hour, but God (the Light) moved by faith toward a new day dawning. When the breakthrough or completion comes, there is always a new day. God calls these breakthroughs or completion times "days."

So through the fourth day of the creation of the heaven and the earth, God has created these things in this manner.

In the first generation, God created:

1. Water.
2. Light.
3. Space.

In the second generation we see these things separated:

1. Light is separated from darkness.
2. Water is separated by a space.

In the third generation, God:

1. Brought the water together under heaven.
2. Caused dry land to appear out of the water.
3. Caused plants to grow out of the land.

In the fourth generation:

1. God created all of earth's solar system.
2. God created everything from the ozone layer out from earth.

Regarding the fifth generation of the creation of heaven and earth, the Scriptures say:

> And God said, Let the waters swarm with swarms of living creatures, and let birds fly above the earth in the open firmament of heaven. And God created the great sea-monsters, and every living creature that moveth, wherewith the waters swarmed, after their kind, and every winged bird after its kind: and God saw that it was good. And God blessed them, saying, Be fruitful, and multiply, and fill the waters in the seas, and let birds multiply on the earth And there was evening and there was morning, a fifth day. (Genesis 1:20–23, American Standard Version)

So on the fifth day, God created all of the water creatures and all of the flying animals throughout the whole earth. The Scriptures also say that He created them after their own kind. He placed the ability to reproduce in every water animal and flying animal. He blessed them and told them to fill the waters of the seas and reproduce in the earth.

One point I want to make right now is that evolution is a lie. It never happened. Every living thing is genetically made with its own DNA. Every living thing has its own chromo-somal structure within every nucleus of every cell.

In fact, the Scriptures say that God made all living things after their own kind and established the seed within each living organism to reproduce after its own kind. Let's look at a scientific belief. This belief is the scientific foundation of all living things, and this scientific foundation is the building block of truth that is explained by the Word of Truth (the Bible). DNA is the seed of all living things within itself, giving it the ability to reproduce after its own kind. It has the flexibility for a variety of characteristics, but maintains the same species.

Microsoft Encarta Encyclopedia has this to say about DNA:

> DNA (deoxyribonucleic acid) is the genetic mate-rial found within the cell nuclei of all living things. These strands of DNA are grouped into structures called chromosomes. With the exception of iden-tical twins, the complete DNA of each individual is unique.
>
> Deoxyribonucleic Acid (DNA), genetic mate-rial of all cellular organisms and most viruses. DNA carries the information needed to direct protein synthesis and replication. Protein synthesis is the production of the proteins needed by the cell or virus for its activities and development. Replication is the process by which DNA copies itself for each descen-dant cell or virus, passing on the information needed for protein synthesis. In most cellular organisms, DNA is organized on chromosomes located in the nucleus of the cell.[19]

In studying different animal structures by mapping the different types of DNA, science has discovered there is very little difference between the numbers of DNA molecules in the nucleus of a cell. The thing that causes each plant and animal to be different is the different types of protein produced by the DNA molecule.

To make a long story short, I believe man is proving the Bible to be the only true way to believe in creation. This very concept shows that what the Bible says is true. The seed of every living thing is within itself. Science is tinkering with the concept of cloning sheep and other animals. All they are really doing is taking the seed out of one cell and planting it in another cell. They are not doing anything but altering the characteristics of the sheep while it is in the one-cell stage (egg just fertilized by sperm). They take the one set of chromosomes out and replace it with another set of chromosomes. The chromosomes are the seeds planted in each and every living thing, seeds that will only produce after their own kind.

Some doctors and scientists believe it is acceptable to alter or kill the newly fertilized egg. They call this egg an "embryo" and a small maturing baby a "fetus." These names are scientific jargon to keep us from seeing the truth. Why? It is called money (greed), convenience (selfishness) to cover sin, and lack of human ability to take responsibility. If science can prove that all the characteristics of a human being are in each cell, how can we allow someone to kill that life just because it hasn't totally formed yet? You can say what you like and believe what you like, but truth is truth. In the end you will have to answer for your own decisions.

There are mutations and adaptations, but every living thing has been designed by God to perform a certain function or service. Not one animal has evolved from another animal. Some have not been able to adapt to a changing environment and have become extinct. Some have had minor adaptations, but they're still the same animal. Each cell divides and has the exact same number of chromosomes as the parent cell.

Every cell comes from the division of a preexisting cell. All the cells that make up a human being, for example, are derived from the successive divisions of a single cell, which is formed by the union of an egg and a sperm (*see* Fertilization). In the process of cell division called mitosis, a new cell arises with an identical number of chromosomes as the parent cell. In mitotic division each chromosome divides into two equal parts, and the two parts travel to opposite ends of the cell. After the cell divides, each of the two resulting cells has the same number of chromosomes and genes as the original cell. Every cell formed in this process thus has the same array of genetic material. Simple one-celled organisms and some multicellular forms reproduce by mitosis; it is also the process by which complex organisms achieve growth and replace worn-out tissue.[20]

For example, a farmer can work with different types of corn to produce a desired trait or resistance to different diseases. It is all still corn that he is crossbreeding. He cannot work with soybeans to improve corn. The farmer looks for traits he likes and concentrates on duplicating this desired characteristic.

Another example would be the thoroughbred racehorse Secretariat. This horse was arguably the greatest thoroughbred horse that ever raced. Secretariat defeated all the horses that ever raced against him. He was amazing. He had speed. He had stamina. He had all of the desired traits of a great racehorse. He was held back in most of his races because the owner, his trainer, and his jockey did not want him to wear himself out early in the race. His jockey never had to use the whip on him. When they finally let him go and run his own race, he destroyed the other horses. He won the last leg of the Triple Crown by more than thirty horse lengths.

He totally destroyed the track time record. When Secretariat died more than twenty-five years later, they cut him open to see if there was anything special about him. He had an extra-large heart and was able to pump blood more quickly and easily than any other horse. Even with this super heart, however, Secretariat was still a thoroughbred racehorse.

This brings us to the last day (generation) of the creation of the heaven and the earth. You might be thinking, *I thought there were seven days of the creation of the heavens and the earth.* It is true. There are seven days (generations) of the creation of the heavens and the earth, but the seventh day is a day of rest. Therefore, the sixth day is the last day of God's labor in creating the heavens and the earth. I will spend more time on this sixth creative period, because there is more written about this day than the other five previous days. This sixth creative period was the day God was moving toward from the beginning when God said, "Let Light be." (Genesis 1:3, 1898 Young's Literal Translation) [21]

And God said, Let the earth bring forth the living creature after its kind, cattle, and creepers, and its beasts of the earth after its kind; and it was so. And God made the beasts of the earth after its kind, and cattle after their kind, and all creepers upon the earth after their kind. And God saw that it was good. And God said, Let Us make man in Our image, after Our likeness. And let them have dominion over the fish of the sea, and over the fowl of the heavens, and over the cattle, and over all the earth, and over all the creepers creeping on the earth. And God created man in His image; in the image of God He created him. He created them male and female. And God blessed them. And God said to them, Be fruitful, and multiply and fill the earth, and subdue it. And have dominion over the fish of the sea and over the fowl of the heavens, and all animals that move upon the earth. And God said, Behold! I have given you every herb seeding seed which is upon the face of all the earth, and every tree in which is the fruit of a tree seeding seed; to you it shall be for food. And to every beast of the earth, and to every fowl of the heavens, and to every creeper on the earth which has in it a living soul every green plant is for food; and it was so. And God saw everything that He had made, and behold, it was very good. And the evening and the morning were the sixth day. (Genesis 1:24–31, Modern King James Version)

I am going to divide this generation into segments or compartmentalize them in the following chapter. We can see that in the sixth day God created human beings and every animal that walks on the face of the earth. God gave Adam dominion over everything that was created. The sixth generation has more written about it in the second and third chapter. There is more information about this generation of creation then any of the other days. The Holy Spirit, the Author of the book of Genesis, reflects back and expands on the sixth day of creation in chapters 2 and 3 of Genesis. Because of this, I am going to explain and show the facts as they are revealed. I am sure you will come to the same conclusion that I have.

Chapter 4

Three Individual Segments of the Sixth Day of Creation

L ooking at each generation on an individual basis makes the book of Genesis come alive. Very little has been taught on Genesis in this modern-day era in which we live. A lot of what has been taught makes no sense. I have heard all kinds of beliefs and ideas about Genesis and how we should interpret this book. We could bring up each individual way of looking at Genesis, or I could go on and write what I see to be the truth. Kenneth E. Hagin, a modern day prophet of God, said it best: "Eat the hay and spit out the sticks." What Kenneth E. Hagin was implying by this statement is that we need to have the common sense of a cow. Eat the hay, and if it doesn't taste good, spit it out. I like hearing new things, but I don't believe everything I hear. We all need to follow after peace and if we do not have peace in our gut then we should put those thoughts on hold until we have time to search out the Scriptures for more insight. If I cannot find confirmation in the Scriptures, then I discard that idea or I put it on the back burner so to speak. You see, in the end when it is all said and done, we only have to answer for what we have done with what we know.

Moving into the sixth creative period of the creation of the heaven and earth, we see that there are three segments of creation within the sixth day (generation). Each one of these three segments was an individual creation period within the whole creation period God calls "the sixth day." Let's look at the first segment of the sixth day.

> And God said, Let the earth bring forth the living creature after its kind, cattle, and creepers, and its beasts of the earth after its kind; and it was so. And God made the beasts of the earth after its kind, and cattle after their kind, and all creepers upon the earth after their kind. And God saw that it was good. (Genesis 1:24–25, Modern King James Version)

What God speaks always happens. In this first segment of the sixth day, God spoke to the earth to bring forth living creatures. Every type of living, breathing creature, cold-blooded and warm-blooded or big and small was created by God in the sixth creative period. When God said, "Let the earth bring forth the living creatures" (Genesis 1:24), God was proclaiming that all of these creatures would be taken and made from the particles of dirt. One could say God took the properties of dirt and manufactured every living thing we see. Please notice that God spoke and they were created. God spoke and life began in each and every animal.

The Scriptures state further that God saw what He created. His opinion of what He had created was good. God didn't say good and evil. The Scriptures say that it was only good. I cannot stress enough how God created everything up to now.

God:

1. Spoke everything into existence.
2. Made everything with the properties to be different.

3. Made everything with the ability to only reproduce
its own kind.

Evolutionists believe everything evolved out of single-
celled animals over billions of years. The book of Genesis
says God created each animal after its own kind. God made
each living thing with its own specific genetic code and gave
it the ability to replicate itself through some form of sexual
activity. There are some forms of life such as the earthworm
that have both reproductive abilities, however these earth-
worms cannot reproduce by themselves; they have to lay
with another worm to reproduce. In all cases it takes the
interaction of the male to transmit seed into the egg of the
female. Plant life requires an outside source like wind, an
insect (for example, a bee), or an animal (for example, a
bird) to transfer the seed. Both male and female have part of
the design within themselves to procreate. Only by mutual
interaction can all living things be replicated by a male and
female. This interaction will always create the same type of
living organism at a cellular level. This single-cell living
organism has the full properties of its adult self when it is
first formed. The beauty of God's creation is the way in
which this single-celled embryo is transformed into a fully
developed adult. This single-celled embryo has all of the
properties of the adult locked into its own individual DNA.

In sexually reproducing organisms the egg cells carry
half of the genetic information of the fertilized individual.
Egg cells constitute the female gametes while the sperm
cells constitute the male gametes. Since these gametes carry
only half of the genetic code, they are termed haploid. The
fertilized egg contains both the genetic contribution of the
male as well as that of the female and is termed diploid.[22]

I can prove that we did not evolve from a single cell
but that we grew from a single fertilized egg. I will use a

simple saying that most people have heard at least once in their lives. Which came first, the chicken or the egg? This question sounds innocent enough, but if you can answer this question, you can disprove evolution. In thinking about the question, you see an egg and the end adult product of that living embryo. The truth of the matter is really simple to answer. The egg could not have been made first because it would have only created one chicken. If the egg hatched and created one chicken, how would it produce after that without a rooster? Therefore God had to create both a chicken and a rooster before one fertile egg could be produced. So how could both the chicken and the rooster evolve into fully developed adult animals from one egg? These one-egged embryos could not evolve into two different sexes (male and female) by accident. It takes both to create one fertile egg. The only possible answer is that God created both and they produce after their own kind. What are the chances of both evolving into a chicken and a rooster to produce one fertilized egg? No wonder evolutionists say we were made over billions of years. If you had a billion years, you could not cause one chicken and one rooster to be accidentally created to produce just one fertilized egg.

God makes His greatest creation in this segment of the sixth day (generation). In this second segment of the sixth generation of the creation of heaven and earth, God does much the same as before:

> And God said, Let Us make man in Our image, after Our likeness. And let them have dominion over the fish of the sea, and over the fowl of the heavens, and over the cattle, and over all the earth, and over all the creepers creeping on the earth. And God created man in His image; in the image of God He created him. He created them male and female. (Genesis 1:26–27, Modern King James Version)

God created man in His own image, and after His own likeness! Think about this statement. We all know what our image looks like in a mirror. Let us look at the meaning of the words *image* and *likeness* in *Strong's Exhaustive Concordance*.

Image
tselem tseh'-lem
from an unused root meaning to shade; a phantom, i.e. (figuratively) illusion, resemblance; hence, a representative figure, especially an idol:—image, vain shew. [23]

Likeness
dmuwth dem-ooth'
from 1819; resemblance; concretely, model, shape; adverbially, like:—fashion, like (-ness, as), manner, similitude. [24]

So God created man in God's own resemblance. Man looked like God. Looking at Genesis 2:7 gives us a more in-depth picture of how He created us.

And Jehovah God [1] formed man of the dust of the ground, and [2] breathed into his nostrils the breath of life; and [3] man became a living soul. (Genesis 2:7, Modern King James Version, numerals added)

We see that God formed man like Him. The very Spirit of God was injected into this flesh (earth) by God's breath, and the Bible says man became a living soul.

1. Formed man of the dust   Body
2. Breathed into his nostrils   Spirit

3. Man became a living soul Soul (mind, will, and emotions)

Every person walking around in this world has a body. The body gives us the right to be in this world. When our spirits leave our bodies, we are dead to this world and can no longer affect this world. You could say that this body (flesh or dust) gives us the ability to be here, just as an astronaut needs a moon suit when he goes to the moon. If he takes off the moon suit, he will not have the ability to be on the moon any more. This body gives us the right or entitles us to be here. One could say that our bodies are the title deeds for this world's occupation.

Every person has a soul. The soul is your mind, your will, and your emotions. Notice that when your spirit man leaves your body at death, the body cannot think anymore. Even though your brain matter is still in your body, that brain matter quits working at death. Most of the people have soul and spirit confused. Some think that they are the same thing. Let's look at the Bible to see what it says about the soul and the spirit.

And may the God of peace Himself sanctify you, and may your whole [1] spirit and [2] soul and [3] body be preserved blamelessly at the coming of our Lord Jesus Christ. (1 Thessalonians 5:23, Modern King James Version, numerals added)

This verse shows three different parts of a person that make up each individual. If we look at it logically, we will see that they are all different. Your soul is not your body, but it is in your body. Therefore your soul cannot be your body. Your soul is also in your spirit, but it is not your spirit. At death your spirit man leaves your body. Your soul goes with your spirit. Your entitlement time is up at death! We have to be ready for the next life at all times, because our entitlement time can be over at any time.

Every person has a spirit. That spirit was given to man through Adam, when God breathed into the body He had formed. Only after the spirit entered the body did man have the capacity to think and reason (become a living soul). The spirit man is the real you. The very breath of God (Spirit) resides within every person. Every person is special to God! We all have the breath of God present in us, because we are all descendants of Adam and Eve. God loves every person equally. God doesn't look at man according to outward appearances. It doesn't matter if:

- ❖ You are good looking or ugly.
- ❖ You are black, yellow, red, or white.
- ❖ You are blind, maimed, or deaf.
- ❖ You only have one leg or arm.
- ❖ You are paralyzed or confined to a wheelchair.

God looks at the heart of man (the inner man).

1833 Webster Bible says:

For there is no respect of persons with God. (Romans 2:11) [25]

The International Standard Version says

For God does not show partiality. (Romans 2:11) [26]

Now we have a good idea how God created man different from all of his other creations. God created Adam like him in all ways. The Scriptures go on to say:

And let them have dominion. (Genesis 1:26)

Strong's Exhaustive Concordance gives us the meaning of the Hebrew word for *dominion*.

radah raw-daw'
a primitive root; to tread down, i.e. subjugate; specifically, to crumble off:—(come to, make to) have dominion, prevail against, reign, (bear, make to) rule,(-r, over), take. [27]

Dominion means "to rule over, prevail against, and to take." So Adam was responsible for everything made from the ground. He was the overseer of everything made from the ground and only the things made from the dirt.

God made us to rule in this environment He created. When God was creating the heaven and the earth in the sixth generation, God created Adam, and God gave Adam leadership over all of His other earthly creations. God gave full authority to Adam in the Garden of Eden over everything made from the dirt. One might say man had authority over all dirt and all creatures made from the dirt. Adam and Eve had complete and total control of everything made from dirt. God placed the earth in both of their care and held nothing back from their authority over the things made of the dirt.

The Modern King James Version gives us added insight into how much authority God gave man.

And out of the ground the LORD God formed every beast of the field, and every fowl of the air, and brought them to Adam to see what he would call them; and whatsoever Adam called every living creature, that was its name. And Adam gave names to all cattle, and to the fowls of the air, and to every beast of the field. (Genesis 2:19–20)

God made the animals and brought them to Adam to be named. So part of Adam's job was to name every animal. This shows that man was in charge of everything made of the ground. Everything God created out of the dust of the ground Adam (man) was in charge of. If you notice, we can travel in space and look at all kinds of dirt. Man brought back samples of the moon. We call them moon rocks. Man will soon have the capacity to blow up an entire planet in space if he had the desire. Kind of scary isn't it? I call that dominion over all things made of dirt.

In Genesis 1:27 we see that God created not only the male but the female also in the sixth generation.

And God created man in His image; in the image of God He created him. He created them male and female. (Genesis 1:27, Modern King James Version)

Now let us look at how God created the female.

But there was not found a suitable helper for Adam. And Jehovah God caused a deep sleep to fall on Adam, and he slept. And He took one of his ribs, and closed up the flesh underneath. And Jehovah God made the rib (which He had taken from the man) into a woman. And He brought her to the man. And Adam said, This is now bone of my bones and flesh of my flesh. She shall be called Woman because she was taken out of man. (Genesis 2:20–23, Modern King James Version)

The first surgery performed on man was by God. So if one's beliefs don't allow surgery or treatment by a doctor, one might need to search the Scriptures. One will find that Luke, one of the four writers of the Synoptic Gospels, was a doctor.

God caused a deep sleep to fall on Adam. How do you think we figured out how to put man to sleep for surgery? God then opened the flesh and removed a rib from Adam's body. This rib that was removed from Adam was made into a woman. One preacher once shared that when Adam was formed from the earth, the Hebrew word for his creation means "he was squeezed." Therefore when Adam was made, God pressure-tested man. God made man tough and durable. But when God made woman, the Hebrew word is different. When God made woman, God handcrafted her. Wow! The man was squeezed, but the woman was handcrafted, delicate and beautiful. The man is Tupperware but the woman is fine China.

This was all done in the period of time God calls the sixth day (generation). We know that because Genesis 1:27 says that God created them male and female during the sixth day of the creation of the heaven and earth. One other major event happened in this sixth generation. This other event that happened in the sixth day was that God created the Garden of Eden. The Garden of Eden did not exist before the sixth day. We know this by what the Scriptures tell us.

And Jehovah God planted a garden eastward in Eden. And there He put the man whom He had formed. (Genesis 2:8, Modern King James Version)

You might be thinking, *How do you know God created the Garden of Eden on the sixth day (generation)? He could have made the Garden of Eden after the seventh day.* The reason you might be thinking this is because the Scriptures tell about all seven days (generations) before the Garden of Eden is even mentioned in the second chapter of Genesis. It is very important to understand the Scriptures. We need to look at this from the viewpoint of the creation of heaven and earth.

1. God created man.
   And Jehovah God formed man of the dust of the ground, and breathed into his nostrils the breath of life; and man became a living soul. (Genesis 2:7, Modern King James Version)

2. God placed man in the Garden of Eden.
   And Jehovah God planted a garden eastward in Eden. And there He put the man whom He had formed. (Genesis 2:8, Modern King James Version)

3. Adam named all of the animals.
   And Adam gave names to all the cattle, and to the birds of the air, and to every animal of the field. But there was not found a suitable helper for Adam. (Genesis 2:20, Modern King James Version)

4. God created woman.
   And Jehovah God caused a deep sleep to fall on Adam, and he slept. And He took one of his ribs, and closed up the flesh underneath. And Jehovah God made the rib (which He had taken from the man) into a woman. And He brought her to the man. And Adam said, This is now bone of my bones and flesh of my flesh. She shall be called Woman because she was taken out of man. (Genesis 2:21–23, Modern King James Version)

We know that God created the male (man) in the sixth day (generation). We know that God created the female (woman) in the sixth day (generation). Therefore God had to have made the Garden of Eden in the sixth day (generation). We can tell this because the details added to the creation of the male and of the female in Genesis chapter 2 include planting (starting) the Garden of Eden.

So in the Garden of Eden, God made the animals and brought them to Adam to be named. So part of Adam's job was to name every animal. This shows that man was in charge of everything made of the ground in the Garden of Eden. Everything God created out of the dust of the ground, Adam (man) was in charge of.

The last segment of the sixth day (generation) is God's direction on eating. God established what Adam and Eve could eat. God also pointed out what the animals could eat. Notice that this is the Garden of Eden diet. Adam's meals consisted of grains, nuts, vegetables, and fruits from trees. I believe this is the origin of only eating nuts, fruits, and vegetables. All of the animals only ate the green plants.

> And God said, Behold! I have given you every herb seeding seed which is upon the face of all the earth, and every tree in which is the fruit of a tree seeding seed; to you it shall be for food. And to every beast of the earth, and to every fowl of the heavens, and to every creeper on the earth which has in it a living soul every green plant is for food; and it was so. And God saw everything that He had made, and behold, it was very good. And the evening and the morning were the sixth day. (Genesis 1:29–3, Modern King James Version)

Meat was not included in the diet for any animal or man in the Garden of Eden. I guess one could say they were on a vegetarian diet. Why was the diet to be all fruits, nuts, and vegetables? I believe it was most likely because to eat meat, something would have to die, but the fruits and vegetables were regenerative. The diet changed when Adam and Eve were separated.

We also can look in the second chapter of Genesis to get further insight into God's direction for Adam's eating habits.

> And Jehovah God took the man and put him into the Garden of Eden to work it and keep it. And Jehovah God commanded the man, saying, You may freely eat of every tree in the garden, but you shall not eat of the tree of knowledge of good and evil. For in the day that you eat of it you shall surely die. (Genesis 2:15–17, Modern King James Version)

Notice that in God's instruction on how to eat, which I believe was given to Adam before Eve was created, Adam was told not to eat from the tree of knowledge of good and evil. Adam could eat from any tree, but he was told not to eat from one tree.

Modern day diets say you are what you eat. We need to have a healthy body so we need to watch what we eat. Dietitians say we need to watch fatty foods, high carbohydrates, red meat, grease intake, fried foods, and many other things. They say you only have one body, so watch what you eat. What we eat can still get us in trouble today. The wrong food choices can cause us health problems, doctors say.

God told Adam not to eat from the tree of the knowledge of good and evil because it would cause severe spiritual and physical health problems. What He told him basically is that you are what you eat. "If you ingest the fruit of this tree, you will take on the characteristics of this tree. I do not want you to take on these traits, therefore do not eat from this tree." Adam was made in the image of God. Adam had all the knowledge of good. If he ate of the tree, then the knowledge of evil would be ingested into his body. God did not want this.

But of the tree[6086] of the knowledge[1847] of good[2896] and evil[7451], thou shalt not eat[398] of it. (Genesis 2:17, King James Version, w/five Strong's Numbers)

Tree
6086 `ets ates
from 6095; a tree (from its firmness); hence, wood (plural sticks):—+ carpenter, gallows, helve, + pine, plank, staff, stalk, stick, stock, timber, tree, wood. [28]

Knowledge
1847 da`ath dah'-ath
from 3045; knowledge:—cunning, (ig-)norantly, know(-ledge), (un-)awares (wittingly). [29]

Good
2896 towb tobe
from 2895; good (as an adjective) in the widest sense; used likewise as a noun, both in the masculine and the feminine, the singular and the plural (good, a good or good thing, a good man or woman; the good, goods or good things, good men or women), also as an adverb (well):—beautiful, best, better, bountiful, cheerful, at ease, X fair (word), (be in) favour, fine, glad, good (deed, -lier, -liest, -ly, -ness, -s), graciously, joyful, kindly, kindness, liketh (best), loving, merry, X most, pleasant, + pleaseth, pleasure, precious, prosperity, ready, sweet, wealth, welfare, (be) well ([-favoured]). [30]

Evil
7451 ra` rah
from 7489; bad or (as noun) evil (natural or moral):— adversity, affliction, bad, calamity, + displease(-ure), distress, evil ([-favouredness], man, thing), + exceed-

ingly, X great, grief(-vous), harm, heavy, hurt(-ful), ill (favoured), + mark, mischief(-vous), misery, naught(-ty), noisome, + not please, sad(-ly), sore, sorrow, trouble, vex, wicked(-ly, -ness, one), worse(-st), wretchedness, wrong. (Incl. feminine raaah; as adjective or noun.). [31]

I believe Adam was already good. In fact, God said after the sixth day (generation) that everything was very good. The key toxic ingredient that this tree bore was evil. God did not want Adam to ingest it. In fact, He did not even want him to touch it. God did not want man to have any part of this tree. So why did God make the tree?

This one prohibition made Adam (man) different from any other created being. Man alone had the freedom to obey God's voice by choice. I believe Adam and Eve were only totally good. They had no conception of disobeying God. They had no conception of evil. They had no conception of death spiritually or physically. Adam and Eve chose how to live their lives in eternality by obeying God's voice.

For in the day[3117] that thou eatest thereof thou shalt surely[4191] die[4191]. (In dieing thou shalt die.) (Genesis 2:17, King James Version, w/three Strong's Numbers)

Notice that the word *die* is used twice. Once it is interpreted as "surely" and the second time it is interpreted as "die."

The Strong's Hebrew and Greek Dictionaries define this word as:

Die
4191 muwth mooth
a primitive root: to die (literally or figuratively); causatively, to kill: — X at all, X crying, (be) dead (body, man, one), (put to, worthy of) death, destroy(-er), (cause to, be like to, must) die, kill, necro(-mancer), X must needs, slay, X surely, X very suddenly, X in (no) wise. [32]

I believe that God is saying to Adam, "Because you will die spiritually, you will also die physically." In dying you will die. All of science is trying to figure out the ageing process. Why does a body that has cells that are continually being replaced age and die? Scientists say that every ten years our bodies have replaced almost all of the cells in our body. So we are not the same group of cells from beginning to end. Our physical body is always changing. Cells are dying and other cells are continually being manufactured to replace them. What causes the ageing processes? Adam's disobedience to God is the root cause of ageing, sickness, death, and disease.

Chapter 5

Setting the Framework and Explaining Genesis 2:4

The first four chapters of this book have set the framework for the rest of the book. We see that God created the heavens and the earth in seven days (generations). Actually, we see that the actual creation time was six generations and that on the seventh day God rested. We are going to look at the Word of God in a new light since we have come this far. I hope that you have enjoyed reading this book as much as I have enjoyed writing it.

Let's take a short review of what we have learned thus far.

1) The first thing God created was light in the first day (generation).
    A) God divided light from darkness.
    a) Light was good.
    b) Darkness was evil.

2) The second thing God created was an expanse called heaven on the second day (generation).
    A) This expanse was placed between water.
    a) Illustrated like this:

Water_____Water

Space   Space

Water_____Water

3) The third day (generation) God caused the water under the space (heaven) to gather together, creating a huge ball (sphere) of water.
> A) God spoke dry land (earth) into existence out of the water.
> B) God created plant life.

4) The fourth day (generation) God created:
> A) The sun to rule (light) the day.
> B) The moon to rule (light) the night.
> C) The stars and planets to light the night.

5) The fifth day (generation) God created:
> A) All flying animals.
> B) All water animals.

6) The sixth day (generation):
> A) God created man and woman in His own image.
> B) God created the Garden of Eden.
> C) Adam was given dominion over all the earth and the living things made from the earth.
> D) Adam named all the animals.

This above is a quick summary of how God created the heavens and the earth. God is very specific in detail about what He created and when He created them. God breaks down these creation segments into generations. We need to look at the Scriptures to see the truth of all of creation. Some people get into all different kinds of thoughts on creation. There have been many books written on different aspects of Christian beliefs. Sometimes good people take in ideas about the creation of heaven and earth without checking these ideas to see what the Scriptures say. To assume or exaggerate an idea without any written proof in the Scriptures is a mistake. Just like saying evolution is true when there are no facts to prove it.

Different people have come up with different ideas throughout the ages. At one time the majority of people thought the world was flat. Anyone who tried to tell them any different would have received the punishment of death. People want to keep things comfortable for their own purposes. In this age of great thinkers we live in, someone once said, "We need to think outside the box." We compartmentalize everything we believe and place those beliefs securely in a place within a box of acceptable thought. If something comes along to test the strength of what we believe, we want to stop it. Most religions have fallen into this trap throughout the ages. If we can't stop the spread of a certain thought, belief, or idea then we will kill it. We have to stop the spread of certain beliefs or we will lose what is in our box. So whatever it takes, we will keep our box intact, even if our box is based on lies and assumptions. We will defend our box to the death. If we don't, we will lose the culture of our ancestors and what they believed and stood for. Fear will grip us, because we see we have to change. We live in the fear of what is outside of the box holding onto what is in our box.

Someone may say that I have my own box. This is true. We all have our own boxes. But my box of belief has been broken open many times by the seeds of truth, and I have had to make a choice each and every time to follow after truth. I am not the same man with the same beliefs of my youth. I have changed. My core values have changed. My beliefs have changed. Religious people have the hardest time looking outside of the box. I will give you an opportunity to look outside of your own box of belief and maybe I already have. It may not hurt the core values of your belief, but it may reorganize your beliefs. You may want to try and stop it, but truth will prevail. Truth will prevail past the graves of man. God is a big God and His ways and thoughts will never be contained within a box.

We have gone through all six days (generations) of creation. We see that the days of creation were finished. God was in a resting mode. The seventh day (generation) was in full swing. God was enjoying the fellowship of His creation (Adam and Eve). Something was about to happen! The temptation of Adam and Eve was about to take place. All of heaven and earth had been created, and God said His creation of heaven and earth was very good. Adam and Eve were enjoying the fruits of God's labor in the Garden of Eden.

Let's look at the King James Version and see what it has to say about this garden.

And the LORD God took the man, and put him into the Garden[1588] of Eden[5731] to dress it and to keep it. (Genesis 2:15, King James Version, w/two Strong's Numbers)

Let's now look at the meaning of *garden* and *Eden* in the Strong's Hebrew and Greek Dictionaries.

1588 gan gan
from 1598; a garden (as fenced): — garden. [33]

5731 `Eden ay'-den
the same as 5730 (masculine); Eden, the region of Adam's home: — Eden. [34]

We see that the Word says that the Garden of Eden was a garden (as fenced) and *Eden* means "the region of Adam's home." So we could translate the above Scripture in Genesis 2:15 like this.

God took the man, and put him into the fenced in protected area [garden] of Adam's original home [Eden]. (Genesis 2:15, author's paraphrase)

This next point is very important for you to understand. Adam and Eve were created in the sixth generation of the creation of heaven and earth. They were created to live forever. They were created in a realm God lives in called eternity. Adam and Eve were made eternal beings. They would not and could not die unless they caused it to happen.

1898 Young's Literal Translation says:

And Jehovah God layeth a charge on the man, saying, 'Of every tree of the garden eating thou dost eat; and of the tree of knowledge of good and evil, thou dost not eat of it, for in the day of thine eating of it—dying thou dost die.' (Genesis 2:16–17) [35]

The Scriptures are plain in stating that if Adam partook of the tree of the knowledge of good and evil in dying (spiritually) Adam would also die in the flesh (physically).

An illustration of Adam's lifeline is:

SPIRITUAL DEATH

E T E R N I T Y (GARDEN)	930 years Genesis 5:5	P H Y S I C A L DEATH

Adam was told by God not to eat of the tree of the knowledge of good and evil. No one knows how long Adam was in eternity before he disobeyed God. It could have been billions of years in our earthly years. In eternity time has no real effect. Time is only relevant to an environment where there is an end (death). One other idea I would like to throw out is that Adam and Eve may have been tempted before. It is not a sin to be tempted. It is sin to give in to your temptations.

As I wrote before, this one prohibition made Adam (man) different from any other created being. Man and woman alone had the freedom to obey God's voice by choice. I believe Adam and Eve were only totally good. They had no conception of disobeying God. They had no conception of evil. They had no conception of death spiritually or physically.

There have been many articles written about this portion of Genesis. To sum them up, Adam was made a free moral agent (possessing free will). He could choose at any time to disobey God. Adam and Eve had the heartfelt desire to please God. They knew they were special to God. God would come and walk and talk with them. This was God's motive for creating Adam (man). This type of relationship is called fellowship. God created the Heaven and Earth and all the contents for his good pleasure. In fact, God called it very good.

God went on and said, "If you eat of this tree you will no longer be an eternal being. You will die! In dying spiritually you will eventually die physically."

Let's return to Genesis 2:4:

These (*days*) are the generations of the heavens and of the earth when they were created. (Genesis 2:4, Modern King James Version, author add *days*)

The first part of Genesis 2:4 is the explanation of what form of day Holy Spirit is revealing to us in the previous seven days. In my opinion God is referring to all of *these* previous days as generations.

> *These* are the generations of the heavens and of the earth when they were created in the day that God made the earth and the heavens. (Genesis 2:4, Modern King James Version)

If we look at the entire verse, we see at first appearance what seems to be a contradiction. The Scriptures will never contradict themselves. This Scripture has two distinct and separate parts. Let's separate them and look at them closely. Understanding this verse is a key to unlocking the first, second, and third chapters of Genesis.

> These (*days*) are the generations of the heavens and of the earth when they were created. (Genesis 2:4, Modern King James Version, author added *days*)

We need to look at one more idea in this portion of the verse. In what order are the words *heavens* and *earth*? *Heavens* is written before *earth*. Right! Heaven is spirit driven. Earth is flesh driven. So when the Scriptures say that these seven days are generations of the creation of the heaven and earth, Spirit is first (heaven) and flesh is second (earth).

> In the day that Jehovah God made the earth and the heavens. (Genesis 2:4, Modern King James Version)

Looking at the second part of this verse, we see earth first and heaven second. This is very interesting to say the least. So we could say that this day (hot time) God made the earth (flesh) first over the heaven (spirit) now second. We could say that this second part of this verse is about man becoming flesh driven over spirit driven. Notice for this meaning of the word *day* I used "hot time" for day. Remember the Hebrew word for *day* means:

1) A hot time.
2) Sunup to sunset.
3) Sunset to sunset.
4) A space of time (large or small).

So we could say this Scripture like this.

These [seven days] are the generations of the creation of the heavens [spirit driven realm] over the earth [flesh driven realm]; in the day [hot time] when God made the earth [flesh driven realm] to come before the heaven [spirit driven realm]. (Genesis 2:4, author's paraphrase)

Another way of saying it from the original Hebrew: Each one of these previous seven days is a historically created generation of the creation of the high and lofty heavens and of the wilderness worldly firm earth; in the day of a hot time or moment of time as is between sunup and sundown the Lord cut down like wood and made flat and made or executed the firm earth to take first place over the lofty, higher, heavenly realm. (Genesis 2:4, author's paraphrase)

A lot of Hebrew scholars say this Scripture is the same instance echoed twice and that God has no preference in what order He places the heaven or the earth, but I believe it does make a difference which comes first. The wording and the word order establishes a difference. In the first part of this Scripture, God is explaining that each one of the creative days were births or generations, explaining everything that preceded that portion of the verse. In the second half of the verse, God shows the preeminence of earth before heaven. After the statement is made in the second half of this Scripture, God begins to explain all of the circumstances that created this day of separation.

God explains how:
1) He made the environment (Genesis 2:5–6).
2) He made man (Genesis 2:7).
3) He made a garden and describes it (Genesis 2: 8–15).
4) He laid down the rules to obey Him (Genesis 2:16–17).
5) He allowed Adam to name all the animals and take authority (Genesis 2:18–20).
6) He created Eve (Genesis 2:21–25).

So we see that this verse in Genesis 2:4 bridges the gap and explains the heaven and earth realm before it and immediately describes the circumstances and rules of that realm. The first part of this verse is talking about the creation of the eternal heaven and earth. The second part of this verse is talking about the creation of the temporary earth and heaven realm. This realm is the realm we see because of Adam's disobedience to God.

Let's look at this day (hot time) in detail.

Chapter 6

The Day of Disobedience

We are going to look at the entire third chapter of Genesis one verse at a time in the Modern King James Version. We are going to look at the Hebrew definitions of important words to clarify the meaning of each verse using *Strong's Exhaustive Concordance*.

> Now the serpent was more cunning than any beast of the field which Jehovah God had made. And he said to the woman, Is it so that God has said, You shall not eat of every tree of the garden? (Genesis 3:1, Modern King James Version)

We need to look in *Strong's Exhaustive Concordance* for the Hebrew meaning of the words s*erpent, cunning, beast,* and *field.*

Serpent
5175 nachash naw-khawsh'
from 5172; a snake (from its hiss): — serpent.[36]

Cunning (subtil)
6175 `aruwm aw-room'

passive participle of 6191; cunning (usually in a bad sense): — crafty, prudent, subtil.[37]

Beast
2416 chay khah'-ee
from 2421; alive; hence, raw (flesh); fresh (plant, water, year), strong; also (as noun, especially in the feminine singular and masculine plural) life (or living thing), whether literally or figuratively: — + age, alive, appetite, (wild) beast, company, congregation, life(-time), live(-ly), living (creature, thing), maintenance, + merry, multitude, + (be) old, quick, raw, running, springing, troop. [38]

Field
7704 sadeh saw-deh'
or saday saw-dah'-ee; from an unused root meaning to spread out; a field (as flat): — country, field, ground, land, soil, X wild. [39]

Looking at these definitions, we see that the snake was a crafty animal. The serpent was cunning in a bad sense more than any other animal in the Garden of Eden. Let's look at what *Easton's Bible Dictionary* says about the serpent.

It has been well remarked regarding this temptation: A real serpent was the agent of the temptation, as is plain from what is said of the natural characteristic of the serpent in the first verse of the chapter (Gen 3:1), and from the curse pronounced upon the animal itself. But that Satan was the actual tempter, and that he used the serpent merely as his instrument, is evident (1.) from the nature of the transaction; for although the serpent may be the most subtle of all the beasts of the field, yet he has not the high intellectual faculties which the tempter here displayed. (2.) In the New Testament it is both directly asserted and in various forms assumed that Satan seduced our first parents into sin (John 8:44; Rom 16:20; 2Co 11:3, 2Co 11:14; Rev 12:9.[40]

I believe *Easton's Bible Dictionary* has a very good explanation of the motivating force behind the temptation of the serpent. One interesting point I would like to point out is how he began his temptation. He asked Eve a question.

And he said to the woman, Has God truly said that you may not take of the fruit of any tree in the garden? (Genesis 3:1, Modern King James Version)

This question was asked in such a way as to bring a strong temptation of eating food. The serpent did not just say eat the food, but he had to get the woman to question what she knew to be true. This question was asked in such a way as to question her knowledge as to what she believed to be true. Let's see what she does.

And the woman said to the serpent, We may eat of the fruit of the trees of the garden. But of the fruit of the tree which is in the middle of the garden, God has said, You shall not eat of it, neither shall you touch it, lest you die. (Genesis 3:2–3, Modern King James Version)

The first thing she did was answer the question. Sounds good! She then elaborated on all of the facts she knew about what she should eat. She said not only could they not eat of that one tree, in addition to this they could not even touch it. If they did either one of these things they would die.

And the serpent said to the woman, You shall not surely die. (Genesis 3:4, Modern King James Version)

The serpent told the woman a lie. "You will not die. God loves you so much that could not happen. Surely you know that," the serpent was telling the woman. Then he sugarcoated that lie by saying, "You shall be as God, knowing good and evil." (Genesis 3:5) Adam and Eve were made in the image of God. Every driving force or desire was to be like God. Their heart cry was to be as godlike as they could be. So when the serpent tempted Eve and Adam, he was moving in an area of their God-given desire, twisting what they knew to be truth. One important point I'm going to make here is, please don't listen to a lie. Do not ever listen to a person who lies. Get away from the person quickly. When people lie, it is always for their benefit, not yours. I have sold cars for more than twenty years and have known sales people and customers to lie about different aspects of a car. Normally, a lie looks like the easier path to follow. But there is always a hook so to speak.

The serpent's statement was a definite lie, and it was specifically targeted. This statement was made to create a question in their minds. The reason I can say this is because Lucifer was one of three Arch Angels. The question was not just expressed by the serpent but it was empowered by one of God's own Angelic Generals. The serpent was the messenger for Satan just like God gave Balaam a message through the donkey. (Numbers 22:25-31) Adam and Eve were beginning to feel uneasy; doubt was entering into their brains. Adam and Eve were made to be faith filled beings controlling the earthly realm. God gave them Dominion (total control). Now with a classic temptation they are beginning to question what God had told them.

For God knows that in the day you eat of it, then your eyes shall be opened, and you shall be as God, knowing good and evil. (Genesis 3:5, Modern King James Version)

The rest of the verse is classic temptation. All temptations follow the path of this Scripture. There are three temptations the devil always uses (1 John 2:16).

1) Lust of the eyes.
2) Lust of the flesh.
3) Pride of life.

And when the woman saw that the tree was good for food, and that it was pleasing to the eyes, and a tree to be desired to make wise, she took of its fruit, and ate. She also gave to her husband with her, and he ate. (Genesis 3:6, Modern King James Version)

Your eyes can fool you. Don't believe everything you see. Such as, that man or woman really looks good. When the woman (Eve) looked at the tree through the eyes of the lie, her desires were impacted. She had to have what she was looking at, and she began to look at the twisted benefits of this tree. The ability to think and dream was placed in us by God. Pornography is a lie that resembles this temptation. Fantasies will spring forth out of your mind and these fantasies will cripple your ability to have a wholesome, godly relationship.

And the eyes of both of them were opened. And they knew that they were naked. And they sewed fig leaves together and made girdles for themselves. (Genesis 3:7, Modern King James Version)

Notice they could see before, because she first used her sight to see the forbidden tree. Once they partook of the tree, their characteristics changed. The Scriptures say that their eyes where opened. Their eyes were opened to evil. The first evidence to evil is lust. Lust will always bring shame. Evil feeds evil. Adam and Eve were not used to looking at each other through evil eyes of disobedience. They had only seen each other through the eyes of a God-breathed being before this moment. Remember, God breathed into Adam. Their bodies (vessels) were only full of godliness. Now they took into their own bodies (vessels) evil. This happened by their own choice of disobedience to what God had told them. They immediately tried to cover themselves. They didn't like the change. They were trying to hide from the guilt of their bad decision. Adam and Eve naturally tried to fix their fallen state. They couldn't undo their disobedience to God, but they tried their best to adjust for their disobedience to God's instructions about eating from this tree. They created a basic problem that is common with humanity today. Adam and Eve tried to cover their disobedience up.

> And they heard the voice of Jehovah God walking in the garden in the cool of the day. And Adam and his wife hid themselves from the presence of Jehovah God in the middle of the trees of the garden. (Genesis 3:8, Modern King James Version)

Hearing God's voice as He walked in the garden, Adam and Eve made another big mistake. When we make a mistake and disobey God, we need to run to Him. The natural thing to do is run from your mistakes. We hide from our responsibilities instead of facing our mistakes head on. We, as creations made in the image of God, need to stand up, get our chins up, and look up. God will deliver us!

Notice God was walking in the garden (fenced in area) of Eden (Adam's original home) in the cool[7307] of the day. Author's interpretation of King James Version w/Strong's number says:

7307 ruwach roo'-akh
from 7306; wind; by resemblance breath, i.e. a sensible (or even violent) exhalation; figuratively, life, anger, unsubstantiality; by extension, a region of the sky; by resemblance spirit, but only of a rational being (including its expression and functions):—air, anger, blast, breath, X cool, courage, mind, X quarter, X side, spirit (-ual), tempest, X vain, (whirl-) wind(-y).[41]

This probably was the first windstorm Adam and Eve ever experienced (an angry tempest). Now that they had a sin-conscious nature fear came upon them, because of their disobedience to the one thing God told them not to do. They no longer felt worthy to be in God's presence. Adam and Eve changed from a faith-filled life to a fear-filled death, and they hid themselves from their Creator among the trees of the garden.

And Jehovah God called to Adam and said to him, Where are you? (Genesis 3:9, Modern King James Version)

Adam and Eve were hiding in the Garden of Eden trying to cover their fallen nature with sewed-together fig leaves. God asked, "Where are you?" This question means more than one thing.

1) God could be asking them where they were positionally (location).
2) God could be asking them where they were mentally and emotionally.
3) God could be asking them where they were spiritually.

I believe God was asking all of the above questions when He asked, "Where are you?" God did not ask this question because He did not know about Adam and Eve's character change. He asked the question to give them the opportunity to confess what they had done.

And he said, I heard Your voice in the garden, and I was afraid, because I am naked, and I hid myself. (Genesis 3:10, Modern King James Version)

Eve was not the one that spoke back to God, because Adam was the spiritual leader. Adam was with Eve when she was tempted, and he should have done something about it. Bad things happen when good people do nothing. Notice that the first expression that Adam made after their disobedience to God was fear. Adam acknowledged that he had heard God; after that he gave his excuse for trying to hide. He said he was naked and because he was naked he had no covering of faith. He only had the covering of fear. Adam and Eve were no longer clothed with the glory of God.

And He said, Who told you that you were naked? Have you eaten of the tree which I commanded you that you should not eat? (Genesis 3:11, Modern King James Version)

God knows everything! Nothing is hidden from God! So why did God ask them these questions? "Who told you that you were naked? Have you eaten of the tree which

I commanded you that you should not eat?" He asked because:

1) God knew all of Adam and Eve's situation.
2) God knew they had lost their eternal life suit (glory-of-God clothing).
3) God knew they now had on an earth suit (death).
4) God knew this suit was inadequate and could not cover their sin (disobedience).
5) God knew that they had eaten of the forbidden tree.

He asked them these questions because God wanted man to begin a form of confession of guilt. The questions God asked Adam opened a pathway of communication through God's mercy and grace. These questions also opened up pathways of excuses and blame shifting. God's questions caused Adam to look hard at what had happened during his watch so to speak. Adam went from a faith-filled successful life to a fear-filled failed life. Adam's core values and beliefs were tainted by the single act of disobedience. Adam and Eve had ingested a lethal dose of disobedience from the tree of evil.

And the man said, The woman whom You gave to be with me, she gave me of the tree, and I ate. (Genesis 3:12, Modern King James Version)

Adam said, "The woman whom You gave to me. It was her fault. She gave me the fruit of the tree that I ate." Adam deflected the blame to the woman. Adam was confessing his guilt before God. Adam was communicating his wrongdoings and Eve's wrongdoings. God was allowing Adam and Eve to build a bridge of communication even though they had disobeyed God's commandment about the tree. God did not have to ask questions, because God had already given Adam and Eve their judgment of death if they disobeyed. But God who is full of love, compassion, and mercy gave Adam and Eve the opportunity to confess what they had done.

> And Jehovah God said to the woman, What is this you have done? And the woman said, The serpent deceived me, and I ate. (Genesis 3:13, Modern King James Version)

God asked Eve, "What is this you have done?" Again God asks a question even though He knew the whole situation. God is getting Adam and Eve to think about what they have just lost. Adam and Eve are being led to confess the sin they had just committed. Again God is building a bridge of hope through their confession of guilt. God is looking at the hearts of Adam and Eve. Only God knows what they need now. God knows that He has opened up a line of communication. God is making Adam and Eve put words to their situation. What is your situation? God is waiting to hear from you! Years and years of stuff might be clogging up the communication with God. God wants to hear from you. He wants to know where you are spiritually, mentally, and physically. He knows! He just wants to hear you put words to your situation. Always remember, the key to any relationship is open, truthful communication. Don't ask a liar questions; it will only cause more lies to be spread about the situation.

> And Jehovah God said to the serpent, Because you have done this you are cursed more than all cattle, and more than every animal of the field. You shall go upon your belly, and you shall eat dust all the days of your life. (Genesis 3:14, Modern King James Version)

Notice God never asked the serpent a question. The serpent was a proven liar! This deceiver lost all credibility with God. God asked both Adam and Eve questions, but to the serpent He spoke what was going to happen. God did not ask the serpent what happened because He knew He would receive a lie. If someone has a history of lying, don't bother to communicate with this person. Communication with a liar will not solve anything. First they have to understand that they are not being honest with themselves. God has no exchange in communication with the serpent. No grace or mercy is shown to the serpent, just judgment. The serpent is told:

1) He is cursed more than any animal of the field. It is assumed that the rest of the things made from the earth were already under the curse of Adam's disobedience. Remember that Adam was given dominion over all the living animals in the garden.
2) The serpent was made to slide on its belly in the dirt.
3) The serpent was forced to eat of the dust of the earth until it died.

All of the living animals were created out of the dirt of the ground, which God created to form out of the water. Because Adam had dominion over all the animals, his disobedience affected all of the animals that God had created. The curse to the snake was additional judgment for its part in Adam's fall from eternal life.

And I will put enmity between you and the woman, and between your seed and her Seed; He will bruise your head, and you shall bruise His heel. (Genesis 3:15, Modern King James Version)

God did not stop with the curse He put on the serpent. He gave Adam and Eve a promise. Genesis 3:15 is one of the most beautiful Scriptures to the entire human race. This one verse holds the key to what God is doing. This verse is the first promise to all of fallen mankind in spite of man's disobedience (sin). God in this sentence basically told the serpent that the seed of the woman would bruise the serpent's head. The serpent may have caused Adam and Eve to stumble because of their disobedience in eating from the tree. But even though it had nipped at their heels and caused them to stumble, God would cause the seed of this fallen woman to bruise the serpent. This word *bruise* means "to be overwhelmed." Therefore we could interpret Genesis 3:15 in this way: "Serpent, you have caused there to be hostility between you and the woman. This hostility will not end with you and the woman. This hostility will continue with your offspring. One day there will be an offspring of this woman who will come and He will bruise (overwhelm) you. You may have caused all of humanity to fall into a sin-conscious dead life because of your lies. You have overwhelmed them enough to entangle and trip them into sin, but the seed of the woman that will come will overwhelm and totally control every part of you forever" (author's paraphrase).

> To the woman He said, I will greatly increase your sorrow and your conception. In pain you shall bear sons, and your desire shall be toward your husband, and he shall rule over you. (Genesis 3:16, Modern King James Version)

In this verse God is saying that there are going to be some additional repercussions because Adam and Eve disobeyed Him. God told the woman she was going to have two types of sorrow. Strong's Hebrew and Greek Dictionaries define both words of *sorrow*.

I will greatly multiply thy sorrow[6093] and thy conception; in sorrow[6089] thou shalt bring forth children. (Genesis 3:16, King James Version w/two Strong's Numbers)

6093 `itstsabown its-tsaw-bone'
from 6087; worrisomeness, i.e. labor or pain:—sorrow, toil. [42]

6089 `etseb eh'-tseb
from 6087; an earthen vessel; usually (painful) toil; also a pang (whether of body or mind): grievous, idol, labor, sorrow. [43]

Both of these Hebrew words are derivatives of this one word.

6087 `atsab aw-tsab'
a primitive root; properly, to carve, i.e. fabricate or fashion; hence (in a bad sense) to worry, pain or anger:—displease, grieve, hurt, make, be sorry, vex, worship, wrest. [44]

Pain, sorrow, labor, and toil are the end results of a disobedient life. Couple that with fear and we see a world that is not very promising. When we live in fear, there is always the fact that the evil in our hearts will keep us captive to our fears.

And to Adam He said, Because you have listened to the voice of your wife and have eaten of the tree, of which I commanded you, saying, You shall not eat of it! The ground is cursed for your sake. In pain shall you eat of it all the days of your life! (Genesis 3:17, Modern King James Version)

Adam listened to his wife's voice and ate from the forbidden tree. God's voice had previously commanded Adam not to eat of this tree. God had told Adam what the circumstances would be if he ate of the tree. Now God adds to the commandment a curse. This curse God says is for Adam's sake. The curse is upon the ground. Every living thing that was under Adam's control was made from the ground. So this curse that was placed on all of mankind was placed on his flesh. In fact, the curse was placed on all things produced from the dirt. The curse on the soil or ground of the earth was for Adam's sake and all of humanity. We will talk about this more as we advance in this book about Genesis.

It shall also bring forth thorns and thistles to you, and you shall eat the herb of the field. (Genesis 3:18, Modern King James Version)

God creates thorns and thistles. God also directs man to eat of the herb of the field.

In the sweat of your face you shall eat bread until you return to the ground, for out of it you were taken. For dust you are, and to dust you shall return. (Genesis 3:19, Modern King James Version)

God's total provision is lost and man is made to work in order to eat. Now man has to fight the weeds of life. Man has to labor long and hard to produce food to eat. Adam is told what is to become of his body. Now that man has died spiritually, man will also die physically. God formed man from the dust of the ground, and when man died physically, his body would go back to dust (dirt).

And Adam called his wife's name Eve, because she
was the mother of all living. (Genesis 3:20, Modern
King James Version)

Adam named his wife Eve. Eve means life giver. The
Scripture states that she is the mother of the human race.
Every person is a descendant of Eve.

And for Adam and his wife Jehovah God made coats
of skins, and clothed them. (Genesis 3:21, Modern
King James Version)

God made a covering for Adam and Eve. They were
naked. God created the clothing industry right here. Adam
and Eve had tied fig leaves together to try to cover their
fallen state, but God made coats from the skin of an animal
to cover them. All animal rights activists take note; the first
clothes made came from the skin (fur) of an animal. This
skin was tailor made by God. It wasn't too big, and it wasn't
too small; the skin was made to fit Adam and Eve's bodies
perfectly. The animal skin was made to help and protect their
fallen bodies. Adam and Eve were now different from how
God had created them. In order to take the skin from the
animal, the animal had to die. Anyone who knows about
separating the skin from the rest of the animal will tell you
that it is a very bloody job. In order for man to be covered in
animal skin for protection, blood had to flow to produce the
covering that God made for Adam and Eve.

And Jehovah God said, Behold, the man has become
as one of Us, to know good and evil. And now, lest he
put forth his hand and take also of the tree of life, and
eat, and live forever. (Genesis 3:22, Modern King
James Version)

God said Adam and Eve were no longer just good, but they also now knew evil because of their disobedient act. Therefore God would have to correct the situation. If God did not do something, Adam and Eve had access to the Tree of Life. If they ate of the Tree of Life, they would live forever in a fallen evil state.

> Therefore Jehovah God sent him out from the garden of Eden to till the ground from which he had been taken. (Genesis 3:23, Modern King James Version)

Therefore God sent them from the Garden of Eden to work the dirt. This dirt is the same kind of dirt that God had formed Adam from.

> And He drove out the man. And He placed cherubs at the east of the garden of Eden, and a flaming sword which turned every way, to guard the way to the tree of life. (Genesis 3:24, Modern King James Version)

The Scriptures say that God forced man out of the Garden of Eden. When He forced Adam and Eve out of the Garden of Eden, He placed angels to guard the way to the Tree of Life. Humanity was kicked out of the eternal realm (heavenly realm) into the dying realm (earthly realm). We need to keep in mind that because of Adam and Eve's disobedience this earthly physical realm we are all born into is just a separated portion of the original creation in the Garden of Eden. What Adam and Eve had dominion over in that realm is what we now see. Notice these facts in the Word of God:

1) Man came to know good and evil.
2) If man had eaten of the Tree of Life in the Garden of Eden, he could have lived forever in a disobedient state (sin).

3) God drove man out of the Garden of Eden. *Eden* means "the region of Adam's home."

4) Man was separated from eternity (eternal life).

5) Man lost his place of his origin (home region).

6) Man died to the things of the heavenly realm (spirit).

7) The reason why God drove man out is to guard the way to the Tree of Life.

8) God placed cherubim (angels) and a flaming sword to keep man out from where he was made.

9) Man had to till or work the ground. This happened to be the same elements his body was made of.

10) Man would no longer have eternal life like God, but now he would die a physical death.

Chapter 7

The Angel Lucifer's Pride

In the first three chapters of Genesis, there is no mention of the devil, Satan, or Lucifer. So how did Lucifer become Satan the destroyer? What was Lucifer's job? Where was Lucifer located? When was Lucifer kicked out of heaven? These are all questions we have asked, plus many more. This chapter covers how Lucifer became Satan. I believe the Holy Spirit has enlightened me in this area. You can be the judge of what I am about to share with you. The Word of God says to "try" or "examine" those to whom you listen.

> Beloved, do not believe every spirit, but try[1381] the spirits to see if they are of God. (1 John 4:1, King James Version w/Strong's Numbers)

Strong's Hebrew and Greek Dictionaries says *try* means:

1381 dokimazo dok-im-ad'-zo
from 1384; to test (literally or figuratively); by implication, to approve:—allow, discern, examine, X like, (ap-)prove, try.[45]

There have been many discussions about when Lucifer became Satan and when Satan was kicked out of heaven. Some people believe Lucifer was kicked out of heaven long before the Garden of Eden was made or before God created the heaven and the earth. Some people believe in a world before Adam where there was a war in heaven and Lucifer was kicked out. The name *Lucifer* means "son of the morning star." The name *Lucifer* is only used one time in all of the Scriptures. This name *Lucifer* pertains to what he was before he tried to proclaim himself as God. Was Lucifer kicked out of heaven as Lucifer? Lucifer's name was changed to Satan in heaven before he was kicked out of heaven. If Lucifer became Satan, how could Satan get back into heaven to be thrown out if Lucifer had already been thrown out of heaven?

The Modern King James Version quotes Jesus as saying:

And He said to them, I saw Satan fall from Heaven like lightning. (Luke 10:18)

If Lucifer was thrown out of heaven sometime before the fall of man, then he could not have been thrown out of heaven as Satan. Therefore Lucifer's name was changed in heaven to Satan before he was thrown out. Lucifer could not have been thrown out of heaven before heaven was created, and Lucifer's name was changed to Satan before he was kicked out of heaven. But as we can see through previous scriptural study, the heaven and earth were in their creation stage, so how could Satan have been thrown out of something that was not created yet? Therefore we cannot say that God cast Satan out of heaven before heaven was created. God did not just create earth. God also created heaven. Genesis chapter 1 is the story of the creation of the heaven and the earth.

The only true way to find out about any topic is by what the Bible says about that subject. If it doesn't fit with what the Bible says, the belief or thought can't be true. The Bible is the Word of God and is always true.

Study earnestly to present yourself approved to God, a workman that does not need to be ashamed, rightly dividing the Word of Truth. (2 Timothy 2:15, Modern King James Version)

If one can rightly divide the truth, then one can wrongly divide the truth. The only way to know if you are wrongly dividing the truth is by personal study. We need to study God's Word (the Bible) and pray for God's direction. The Bible says:

But if any of you lacks wisdom, let him ask of God, *who* gives to all liberally and with no reproach, and it shall be given to him. (James 1:5, Modern King James Version)

So the Bible says if we lack wisdom, ask for wisdom. God will give wisdom to us in abundance. Father God, we ask you to open our eyes to the understanding of your Word. Help us to see the truth about Satan.

Remember, the first chapter of Genesis is about the creation of the heaven and earth. Not just the creation of the earth. So we must say that God is creating heaven, and God is creating earth. Lucifer tried to ascend into heaven the Bible says.

This means that heaven was created before Lucifer tried to ascend up to the heavens.

How art thou fallen from heaven, O Lucifer, son of the morning! how art thou cut down to the ground, which didst weaken the nations! For you have said in your heart, I will go up to the heavens, I will exalt my throne above the stars of God; I will also sit on the mount of the congregation, in the sides of the north. I will go up above the heights of the clouds; I will be like the Most High. (Isaiah 14:12–14, underline added, Modern King James Version)

Lucifer was cast out of heaven according to Isaiah 14:12. As we have seen, Genesis chapter one is about the creation of heaven and the earth. Then heaven had to be created before Lucifer could possibly try to ascend into heaven. How could Lucifer ascend into something that was not yet created?

Let's look at an example. I am building a house. I go out to the location where I am going to place the structure. I take the contractor out to the location. I explain to him that I want a two-story home with a full basement. We walk the ground and get a general lay out of the property. He takes my ideas to an architect. The architect puts our plans on several sheets of paper. We all go out to the location to visualize our plans. Can I go into the second story at this point? No! Why? The house has not been built. Can I go into the house? No! Why? The house has not been built. The house has a foundation to be poured and a basement to be made of concrete. The first thing I have to do is dig a hole in the ground. So I dig a hole in the ground. I am not throwing the ground out of my basement. I am clearing the dirt out of a hole in the ground where I will put my house. Throwing this dirt out of the hole in the ground is not throwing dirt out of my house. I cannot discard anything out of my house until my house is complete or finished.

Heaven and earth were under construction until after the sixth day (generation) of the creation of heaven and earth.

Therefore Lucifer could not have been in heaven until it was finished being built.

> And God saw everything that He had made, and behold, it was very good. <u>And the evening and the morning were the sixth day</u>. (Genesis 1:31, Modern King James Version, underline added)
> And the **heavens** and the **earth** were <u>**finished**</u>, and all the host of them. (Genesis 2:1, Modern King James Version, underline and bold type added)

I believe Ezekiel 28:13 is written about Lucifer. I believe he was made to be the protector of the Garden of Eden. Lucifer's name is never mentioned in this Scripture, but "the anointed cherub that covers" is mentioned. I believe Lucifer was the anointed covering cherub written about in this Scripture. We know Lucifer was an angel made by God who was in a key position in heaven. If you believe this Scripture to be about Lucifer, then you would have to say Lucifer was in the sixth day (generation) of the creation. Therefore, he could not have been thrown out prior to this time could he? Remember, the Garden of Eden was not complete until the sixth period of creation was finished.

> You have been in Eden the garden of God; every precious stone was your covering, the ruby, topaz, and the diamond, the beryl, the onyx, and the jasper, the sapphire, the turquoise, and the emerald, and gold. The workmanship of your tambourines and of your flutes was prepared in you in the day that you were created. You were the anointed cherub that covers[5526], and I had put you in the holy height of God where you were; you have walked up and down in the midst of the stones of fire. (Ezekiel 28:13–14, King James Version, w/ Strong's Number)

Lucifer was the anointed covering cherub. The word *covers* in *Strong's Exhaustive Concordance* means:

5526 cakak saw-kak'
or sakak (Exod. 33:22) saw-kak'; a primitive root; properly, to entwine as a screen; by implication, to fence in, cover over, (figuratively) protect: — cover, defence, defend, hedge in, join together, set, shut up.
[46]

I believe Lucifer's job or position was to protect the Garden of Eden from harm. I believe he was placed as the covering cherub to protect Adam and Eve. Lucifer was the protection or covering of the Garden of Eden.

I personally believe that God created Lucifer as the angel of light during the first three days (generations) of the creation of the heaven and earth. Remember, he is called "the son of the morning star." I cannot prove this theory about Lucifer by the Word of God, so I can only state this as a thought. I also believe God created other things that we don't see. The things we see are the things made from the dirt (earth).

Instead of protecting Adam and Eve in the Garden of Eden, Lucifer launched a scheme of deceit. Lucifer saw all that Adam and Eve had. Adam and Eve had dominion over everything that God made from the dirt. If it was not made from the dirt, Adam did not have dominion over it in the Garden of Eden. Adam and Eve had it made, so to speak. They were perfect in every way. They were eternal beings. They were full of goodness. They were made in the image of God Almighty. Adam had dominion over every animal in the Garden of Eden, including the serpent. Lucifer wanted more than to be a protector over the Garden of Eden. Lucifer was created very bright, beautiful, and wise, but Lucifer wanted to be God!

Although the Scriptures don't say specifically that Lucifer was the covering cherub of the Garden of Eden, most people believe this Scripture is about Lucifer.

Thou wast in Eden, the garden of God; every precious stone was thy covering, the sardius, the topaz, and the diamond, the beryl, the onyx, and the jasper, the sapphire, the emerald, and the carbuncle, and gold: the workmanship of thy tabrets and of thy pipes was in thee; in the day that thou wast created they were prepared. (Ezekiel 28:13, American Standard Version)

Notice the angel who was called "the covering cherub" was in the Garden of Eden. Eden means "the place where Adam was created, Adam's home." Remember, heaven and earth was not completed until the sixth day (generation) was finished.

Isaiah and Ezekiel are both prophetic books. Meaning that at the time these books were written, Isaiah and Ezekiel saw into the future what was going to happen. They did not have to understand all that they wrote, but the power of the Holy Spirit came upon them to write. They were called "seers." Some things they wrote about had already happened; other things were in the process of happening or were going to happen in the future. This ability to write down or speak out what is going to happen in the future is called a prophetic word. These people cannot turn this ability on or off as they want. But when the Holy Spirit gives them a message, they write it down or speak it out. Many people try to manufacture things of God. We need to be very careful about trying to drum up some event. God events will happen, if you seek Him with all of your heart.

Moreover the word of Jehovah came unto me, saying,
Son of man, take up a lamentation over the king of
Tyre, and say unto him, Thus saith the Lord Jehovah:
Thou sealest up the sum, full of wisdom, and perfect
in beauty. (Ezekiel 28:11–12, American Standard
Version)

Take up a lamentation (as beating the breast) against the
king (ruler) of Tyre (rock). I believe "Tyre" represents the
earth (flesh). Tell this ruler of Tyre (rock or earth) this, that
you were stamped with the seal of perfection, of complete
wisdom and perfect beauty.

Thou wast in Eden, the garden of God; every precious
stone was thy covering, the sardius, the topaz, and
the diamond, the beryl, the onyx, and the jasper, the
sapphire, the emerald, and the carbuncle, and gold:
the workmanship of thy tabrets and of thy pipes
was in thee; in the day that thou wast created they
were prepared. (Ezekiel 28:13, American Standard
Version)

This ruler of the rock was in Eden (Adam's home) the
garden (fenced in area) of God. This king of Tyre (earth
or rock) was in Adam's home area. He was very beautiful
with lots of jewelry. This king (Lucifer) had to have been in
Adam's home area. So Adam had to have been made before
this king (Lucifer) of the rock (earth) was cast out. Now let
us find out who this king was that Ezekiel was making a
lamentation against.

Thou wast the anointed cherub that covereth: and I
set thee, so that thou wast upon the holy mountain of
God; thou hast walked up and down in the midst of

the stones of fire. (Ezekiel 28:14, American Standard Version)

Now this king Ezekiel is talking about is a covering cherub. *Covering cherub* means "a protector like a net of out stretched wings." So Ezekiel is not talking about a man but an angel with a lot of power. Lucifer! This cherub was on the holy mountain of God, walking among the fiery stones.

Thou wast perfect in thy ways from the day that thou wast created, till unrighteousness was found in thee. (Ezekiel 28:15, American Standard Version)

You could translate this verse: "Blameless you were in your conduct from the day you were created, until evil was found in you. You then lost your right standing with God" (Ezekiel 28:15, author's paraphrase). This cherub (Lucifer) became unrighteous to God. When Lucifer's desire was not to please God anymore or obey what God's desire was for him, then Lucifer became unrighteous to God. Lucifer lost his right standing with God's direction for his life and became opposed to God. Lucifer was made perfect, but his desire to have more control and more power drove him into a position of absolute opposition to the one who made him in the first place, God.

Ezekiel 28:12–15 is describing Satan's heavenly position, how he was made, and what his position was until he lost righteousness. This is the description of the covering cherub Lucifer, how he was made, and what he was like before he became unrighteous. Then his name was changed to Satan or the devil. Lucifer, which means "morning star in its brightness," was the covering cherub (protector). This covering cherub (Lucifer) became Satan, which means "to lie in wait," or the devil, which means "destroyer."

Ezekiel 28:16–19 is about what is going to happen to Satan. These Scriptures tell us Satan's future. They are seeing into the future about what is coming. This is the devil's future and there is nothing he can do about it. It is written!

By the abundance of thy traffic they filled the midst of thee with violence, and thou hast sinned: therefore have I cast thee as profane out of the mountain of God; and I have destroyed thee, O covering cherub, from the midst of the stones of fire. (Ezekiel 28:16, American Standard Version)

By the abundance of your merchandise and gifts you possess. They have filled thy midst with violence, and you sinned, and I will throw you out of the mountain of God, and I will totally destroy you who were the protecting angel. You will be destroyed from the middle of the stones of fire.

Thy heart was lifted up because of thy beauty; thou hast corrupted thy wisdom by reason of thy brightness: I have cast thee to the ground; I have laid thee before kings, that they may behold thee. (Ezekiel 28:17, American Standard Version)

Your heart was lifted up because you were beautiful; you made your wisdom evil through your disobedience to your purpose for your existence. I have sent you down to the earth; I have made you low before kings, so that they may see you.

By the multitude of thine iniquities, in the unrighteousness of thy traffic, thou hast profaned thy sanctuaries; therefore have I brought forth a fire from the midst of thee; it hath devoured thee, and I have turned thee to ashes upon the earth in the sight of all them that behold thee. All they that know thee among the peoples shall be astonished at thee: thou art become a terror, and thou shalt nevermore have any being. (Ezekiel 28:18–19, American Standard Version)

Now let's look at what Isaiah has to say about Lucifer. Isaiah and Ezekiel are both prophetic books. Therefore some of the things that they were writing about in their books had not happened, but they were going to happen. They were foretelling or giving an insight into what was going to happen.

How art thou fallen from heaven, O Lucifer, son of the morning! How art thou cut down to the ground, which didst weaken the nations! (Isaiah 14:12, King James Version)

In what manner have you fallen from heaven, Lucifer, son of the morning? How are you cut down to the ground (earth or dirt)? You are the one who weakened the nations.

For thou hast said in thy heart, I will ascend into heaven, I will exalt my throne above the stars of God: I will sit also upon the mount of the congregation, in the sides of the north. (Isaiah 14:13, King James Version)

For you Lucifer said in your heart, I will lift myself up and improve my position in heaven. I will put my throne above the stars of God. I will exalt myself above God and His stars. I will also position myself upon the high mountain of the assembly on the edge of the north (dark gloomy hidden unknown part).

I will ascend above the heights of the clouds; I will be like the Most High. (Isaiah 14:14, King James Version)

I will ascend above the heights of the clouds; I will make myself like the Most High. This is what Lucifer said. Notice this tense, Lucifer is speaking in the future or something he wants to do.

Yet thou shalt be brought down to hell, to the sides of the pit. (Isaiah 14:15, King James Version)

The Word of God answers back. Even though you say and think this, you shall be brought down to hell, to the sides of the pit. Notice Isaiah is writing by the Spirit of God about what is going to happen in the future to Lucifer.

They that see thee shall narrowly look upon thee, and consider thee, saying, Is this the man[376] that made the earth to tremble, that shook kingdoms? (Isaiah 14:16, King James Version)

Strong's Exhaustive Concordance says this word *man* means:

376 'iysh eesh
contracted for 582 (or perhaps rather from an unused root meaning to be extant); a man as an individual or a male person; often used as an adjunct to a more definite term (and in such cases frequently not expressed in translation): — also, another, any (man), a certain, + champion, consent, each, every (one), fellow, (foot-, husband-)man, (good-, great, mighty) man, he, high (degree), him (that is), husband, man(-kind), + none,

one, people, person, + steward, what (man) soever, whoso(-ever), worthy. Compare 802. [47]

I believe this word should have been interpreted *champion* not *man*.

That made the world as a wilderness, and destroyed its cities; that opened not the house of his prisoners? (Isaiah 14:17, King James Version)

Satan destroyed the world and laid it to waste. Satan let no prisoners free. He held the earth captive.

All the kings of the nations, *even* all of them, lie in glory, everyone in his own house. But thou art cast out of thy grave like an abominable branch, *and as* the raiment of those that are slain, thrust through with a sword, that go down to the stones of the pit; as a carcass trodden under feet. Thou shalt not be joined with them in burial, because thou hast destroyed thy land, *and* slain thy people: the seed of evil-doers shall never be renowned. (Isaiah 14:18–20, King James Version)

So how did this great angel (Lucifer) fall into destruction and sin?

This is my belief regarding how it happened. Lucifer was the covering cherub in the Garden of Eden. Adam had dominion over everything made from the earth. Lucifer was a covering protector of everything in the Garden of Eden not in charge but placed by God to be the light. Lucifer like all angels was not made of the earth. The Bible said he controlled one third of all the angels. Lucifer was beautiful, powerful, musical, and wise. That was not enough for him.

He put together a scheme to steal control from Adam and set himself up to be like God. Adam was made in the image of God but Lucifer wanted what power Adam had and more. In his prideful mind, he was going to be like God. Because he was a spiritual being (not made of the earth), he was different from the creations made of the earth (dirt). Lucifer put together a plan. Lucifer called on the serpent. He told the serpent to go to the woman and ask her a question. Why? Lucifer wanted the control over all of the things made of the earth (dirt). If Lucifer could get man to do the one thing he was not supposed to do, then he would cause Adam to give up his power over all things made of the flesh. Adam would then be subject to Lucifer because of his temptation plan. Lucifer had to find the right animal that was persuasive and subtle enough to be the right influence in a charming way. This message had to be said with the right wording just to create a thought of doubt. This little seed of doubt about God would cause Adam and Eve to bow their knees to Lucifer and be subject to him.

> Now the serpent was more subtle than any beast of the field which the LORD God had made: and he said to the woman, <u>Yea, hath God said, Ye shall not eat of every tree of the garden?</u> (Genesis 3:1, underline added, King James Version)

This question opened up a dialog for Lucifer to become the god of all the things made of the flesh. This question planted the idea in Eve's mind, *You're missing out on something. God is leaving you out. God is not being fair to you because He is keeping you from something.* This question is asked with precision to cause doubt to come into Adam and Eve. I say Adam and Eve because Adam was with her. Adam had dominion over the situation and should have stopped the serpent. The serpent was made of the earth and was under the authority of Adam. Adam should have stopped the conversation. Adam was in charge and watched as Eve was sucked into a conversation of evil intent. This suggestion caused the temptation to grow in their minds. Fantasies grow by suggestions as emotions get sucked into the thought processes. The question was a statement of fact. There was one tree in the entire garden that they were told not to eat of. This one single tree gave them the ability to choose to follow God. If God had not given them this choice, they would have been like puppets on a string. This one prohibition made them special in the eyes of God.

Adam and Eve were made full of faith and goodness. Their hearts' cry was to obey the voice of God. They were made eternal beings with the covering of God's righteousness. They walked and talked with God. Adam and Eve were like a king and queen in their earthly domain. Everything made of the dirt of the ground was under Adam and Eve's rule. They were like gods over the things made of the earth. This power and authority was a temptation to the covering cherub Lucifer. He began to feel that he desired to be the ruler over this kingdom. If God would not give it to him, he would take it from Adam. Lucifer was not made to have a freedom of choice. He was an angel designed for a purpose. Lucifer was filled with wisdom and beauty.

I believe Lucifer was one of the three most powerful angels. And I believe each one of these angels was in charge of one third of the angels of God. These angels were called *archangels*, and their names were Lucifer, Gabriel, and Michael.

Lucifer means "the bright and morning star."
Gabriel means "the man of God."
Michael means "who is like God?"

Lucifer had an army of angels to control, but that was not enough. Lucifer saw the flexibility and freedom of control God had given to Adam in the Garden of Eden. Lucifer was beginning to desire (lust) after what Adam had. After all, Adam had an equal partner, his helper (Eve), who completed him. Lucifer had nothing like that! Sure, Lucifer was made to be a protector and given power over one third of the armies of God. Lucifer began to look at the things he didn't have rather than at the things he had. The very powers of sin gave birth in an angel called Lucifer. One of these three characteristics is always present with the beginning phase of all temptation. (1John 2:16)

1. The lust of the eyes.
2. The lust of the flesh.
3. Pride of life.

All three of these earthly desires are present when we are tempted to disobey God. The "lust of the eyes" could be stated as the "lust of the senses." If a person were blind, his sense of touch, smell, taste, and hearing would be impacted in the same way.

Lucifer needed an animal to be used as a servant for his cause. I believe the reason that Lucifer needed an animal to tempt Adam was because Adam had dominion over all of the animals. If Lucifer could influence Adam who was in charge over all things made of the earth through one of the things made from earth, then he could grab control from Adam. The serpent was the animal of choice because of its crafty personality. The serpent should not have listened to Lucifer at all, because Adam was in control of the serpent not Lucifer. The serpent's temptation was rebellion against the authority of Adam, and this rebellion was against the desire of God. I believe in the back of the serpent's mind, he thought, *I am going to increase my stature. I will make myself some-*

thing special by my own crafty gifts. I will take upon myself more power because of my own ability. He agreed with the angel Lucifer, because the seed of rebellion against God was planted in him through Lucifer. Some may say, "Why was Eve talking to a snake in the Garden of Eden? When did a snake ever talk to one of us?" We need to remember that these events took place in the Garden of Eden before Adam and Eve gave in to sin (disobedience to God's commandment). The serpent or dragon is still the animal that is used to represent the devil because this animal was his representative to take control of Adam's kingdom.

Lucifer became so delusional that he wanted to be what he never could be. God! In his own wisdom he became prideful. As he was lifted up in pride because of his looks and wisdom, he began to fantasize about himself. Adam's commandment became Lucifer's temptation for more power. I believe Adam would never have sinned in the Garden of Eden without the supernatural influence of the angel Lucifer using the serpent as a pawn. Lucifer changed in every way. He was no longer protector. He was destroyer! When he changed, he took rebellious control of one third of the angels of God. God changed his name forever. From this time forward, God calls Lucifer "Satan." His purpose is forever changed. God the Creator begins to speak into existence Satan's future. God formulates a plan hidden from the foundations of the earth. A deliverer will be sent to this fleshly ruled world to undo the atrocities of this undeserving tyrant Satan.

Chapter 8

The Promise Hidden from the Foundation Revealed

The key to unlocking the truth about the creation of the heaven and earth is located in Genesis 2:4.

> (1) These are the generations of the heavens and of the earth when they were created, (2) in the day that the LORD God made the earth and the heavens. (Genesis 2:4, King James Version, numerals added)

This verse is two statements of truth about creation. The first statement is about the creation of the heavens and earth. The second statement is about the creation of the earth and heavens. I numbered them so you could see the two statements. If you just read the verse, you might think it is a contradiction, but when you look closely, you see differences. The first statement is talking about generations of creations. The second statement is talking about a sudden change. If we look at the Scripture in detail, we see heaven and earth being flipped around. Heaven is mentioned first in the first statement. Heaven is mentioned last in the second statement. Earth is mentioned last in the first statement and earth is mentioned first in the second statement. *Heavens* represents the spiritual world and *earth* represents the physical world. In the first statement the Word of God is talking about the creation of a spirit-first world and the second statement is talking about the start of a flesh-first world.

1. Heavens (spirit first)   Earth (flesh next)
2. Earth (flesh first)   Heavens (spirit next)

The first part of this verse is about the creation of the heavens and earth as God made them perfect in every way. God made all the wonders of the spirit world and of the earthly world to exist in perfect harmony. This world coexisted in balance and majestic beauty. It was made perfectly and without a blemish. This created environment was empowered by God and guided by the Spirit of God. This world is eternal. This world took generations to perfect its completion. In this world the Spirit of God guided all life. This world we can no longer see; it is hidden from us because of Adam and Eve's disobedience (sin).

The second part of this verse is talking about the creation of earth and heavens. This world is flesh guided. This world is under the rules of the flesh and it is plagued with the promise of death. This world was made in an instant of a disobedience-guided life. When Adam and Eve ingested the fruit from the tree of disobedience, this world began. This world is the world we see, because we only see the things made from the earth. The curse came to humanity by the power of the flesh. This world is flesh ruled. The things we know, see, and do are revealed to us through the senses of our flesh.

Therefore "the creation of the heavens and earth" mentioned in Genesis 1:1–2:3 is about the creation of all things by God in their original forms. This creation was perfect in every way. This place was a God-directed eternal world. Male and female were created never to die. They were molded from the earth, but they were guided by the things of the Spirit of God. Everything was in perfected harmony. Some ministers have even preached how that Adam and Eve were covered and clothed with the Glory of God. Man was living in a place called the Garden of Eden. There was no rain, just a mist from the earth.

> God had not caused it to rain on the earth. . . . But there went up a mist from the earth, and watered the whole face of the ground. (Genesis 2:5–6, King James Version)

A river watered the Garden of Eden, and this river split into four other rivers. In the original creation, there were all kinds of gold and jewels in the area of these rivers. Adam and Eve lived in perfect harmony with all other things made from the dirt (earth). I can only imagine how the earth must have been in its original created form. This environment was multifaceted and much more complex than the simple three-dimensional world we now see.

> And the LORD God said, Behold, the man hath become as one of us, to know good and evil. And now, lest he should put forth his hand, and take also of the tree of life, and eat, and live forever: Therefore the LORD God sent him forth from the garden of Eden, to till the ground from which he was taken. So he drove out the man: and he placed at the east of the garden of Eden Cherubim, and a flaming sword which turned every way, to keep the way of the tree of life. (Genesis 3:22–24, King James Version)

These three verses are the description of the second statement in Genesis 2:4. It explains what happened after Adam and Eve disobeyed God's desire for their life. Notice the words "behold the man has become as one of us." I do not believe the general belief that God was talking about Himself or the Godhead. I believe He was talking about every living being in the Garden of Eden or in the present realm of God's existence. The Garden of Eden was the place in which the heavenly (Spirit) realm ruled. Let's look at a story type example to explain what I believe the Scripture is saying here:

Three guys are in this newly started heavenly enterprise called the Tree of Life Inc. These guys were handpicked because of their expertise in their fields of work. Their Boss, the Big Guy, hired them! Their Boss, the soul proprietor you could say, created every one of them. They were made to be presidents of their departments as the enterprise grew, and each one of them was in charge of one third of the company's employees. These employees were so perfect, one could call them angels. Their Boss had so much faith in their ability to perform that he gave them total control over every employee under them. I guess you could say these presidents totally owned all of the employees (angels) under them. In fact, these employees were so loyal to their presidents that they acted just like them in every way. If the president in charge of them wore a double-breasted suit, all of the employees would go get themselves one because they wanted to be just like their president. Whatever he ate, they would eat. Whatever their president would do, they would do. Their president was their total and complete role model. These employees took on the characteristics of their presidents in every area of their lives, good and bad. These three presidents only had first names. Their names were Michael, Gabriel, and Lucifer. They were so good at their jobs that the Big Guy called them archangels most of the time instead of presidents. Everything went smoothly until this president by the name of Lucifer began to get some bad habits. He started looking in the mirror too much. He began to think about how beautiful he was and how perfect he was. He began to fantasize how great it would be to own the business. You can see all the problems that began to happen, because all of the employees under him began to do the same things.

The Big Boss had a special customer that was a spitting image of his own person who was named Adam. Of all the customers, there was no customer that the Big Boss wanted to keep more than Adam. The Big Boss had given Lucifer Adam's account. The Big Guy expected Lucifer to take excellent care of Adam. Lucifer became jealous of Adam, because he got most of the Big Boss's attention. So this president (Lucifer) launched a scheme to steal the customer from the Big Guy. Lucifer told Adam about a new venture called the Tree of Evil Inc. Adam and his wife Eve had heard about this business, but had always believed that this was a bad investment. The Big Guy had warned Adam and Eve about the product; he said it would cause death. Lucifer got the snake, one of the craftiest critters in the Big Guy's garden, to present his business opportunity. Lucifer picked the snake because he could sell anything to anybody, even if he had to lie to get the sale. Lucifer saw an opportunity to be his own boss and be a big guy too in the Tree of Evil Inc. business. The snake succeeded in getting Adam and Eve to buy into this new ground floor corporation and consume the product. Adam and Eve took on the evil characteristics of this evil fruit-bearing tree.

The Big Boss held a special corporate meeting and invited his presidents to attend and gave a special invitation to Adam. The Big Boss began the meeting by explaining to his favorite customer what had happened. He looked at Adam and said; "You know you used to be like Me, but now you're acting like one of us in this garden (Lucifer). I am going to have to change the way we do business for your own good, Adam. Not only did I want your business, but I was also looking toward the future, and I wanted your children's business also. There is one problem though; you are not acting like Me anymore; you are acting like Lucifer now. So I am going to take you away from the Tree of Life product. You and your children will die, but one day one of your offspring, a lady just like your wife, is going to have a Son. This Son will correct the bad behavioral patterns you now have because of my president Lucifer's influence. This man born of a woman will obey My voice and will totally give of Himself to undo this Tree of Evil Inc. business. He will totally bring to an end the death brought on by this business and show the way to renew the Tree of Life Inc. business. "

And the Big Guy said to Lucifer, "I don't like your business practices. They are going to burn, but first I am going to change your job title. Your name is no longer Lucifer. From this day forward, you will be called "the deceiver" (the Satan) or "the destroyer" (the devil). Your employees are no longer acting like angels because of you, Satan. Now they are acting evil like you have become. Therefore, from this day forward they are called demons. Eventually, I will totally throw you and your demons out of My business, but for Adam's sake I will hold my wrath against you until I can free Adam and his offspring from you and your demon authority over them. When my Son comes through the birth of one of Adam's offspring, He will take back the authority from you and smash your head. Then my Son will reestablish good business practices and break down communication barriers. When He does, I will bring together a group of investors, who will prayerfully listen to Me. These people, led by my Son and comforted by a third owner's presence in their lives (the Holy Spirit), will totally destroy you, Satan, and your copycat fallen demons. Then I will totally restore to Adam and his offspring who obey Me and My Son their rights to eat of the Tree of Life Inc. forever." (Authors story)

Adam and Eve were driven out of the Garden of Eden because God didn't want them to eat from the Tree of Life. There is now a barrier between eternity and this present world we now see. God placed two angels to guard the way to the Tree of Life.

What does all this mean? Is there a hope? Who is this hope? How do I know the truth? Where is the Son? We have studied the creation of the heaven and the earth. We have seen the downfall of man, which brought physical death into the world. We have seen how God created all things and drove man from the Garden of Eden. If I leave you at this point, you will be most miserable. You have now seen the truth of creation. We all have the same roots. We all have the same birthright through Adam and Eve. The breath of God has been transferred from generation to generation and here we are, men, women, and children of the Most High with one problem. We all are separated from our Creator. We all will die a physical death. We all need help to correct what Adam and Eve had lost.

The Jewish believer is looking for the Messiah to come. The Muslim is following the ways of Muhammad.

The Christian is waiting for the return of Jesus. We are all waiting, but what are we all looking for? Why do we believe what we believe? Are there any other life-forms on any other planets?

The first three chapters of Genesis don't give us the answers to all of these questions, although they do give us enough information to draw some interesting conclusions. For instance, I do not see Muhammad or a connection to Muhammad in any of these chapters. I only see one Messiah who measures up to the first three Chapters in Genesis 1-2-3. So some people must have their thinking mixed up. All religions can't be right, because they disagree on too many things. I will not measure all of the different beliefs, but I will tell it like it is. All three believe the book of Genesis is a message to us from God. Muslims reject the teaching of Genesis and repositions their focus on a more recent belief or prophet. This is always the road to being deceived: to put your arms around something in belief and then redirect the focus to a later, more up-to-date book. Why do I say this? Because if Muslims studied Genesis, they would see the truth, and if they saw the truth, they would reject the religion of their natural fathers and look to the Creator of the universe our heavenly Father. This may sound to you as if I am writing very boldly. I defy you to be strong enough to check out what I am writing about.

The true Christian believes all of the Scriptures contained in the Bible are the Word of God. Christians believe that:

> In the beginning was the Word, and the Word was with God, and the Word was God. The same was in the beginning with God. All things were made by him; and without him was not any thing made that was made. (John 1:1–3, King James Version)
>
> And the Word was made flesh, and dwelt among us, (and we beheld his glory, the glory as of the only

begotten of the Father,) full of grace and truth. (John 1:14, King James Version)

1. God and His Word are one.
    A) One in purpose.
    B) One in vision (direction).
    C) One in truth.
    D) One in life.

2. This Word of God became man in the flesh (John 1:14).
    A) His name was Jesus.
    B) He was born in Bethlehem (Micah 5:20).
    C) He was raised in Nazareth (Isaiah 11:1).
    D) He was baptized by John.
    E) His title is Christ (Anointed One or Messiah).

Some of you may not see the truth yet, but I dare you to open your minds to the possibility of what I am writing. Notice that "the Word was made flesh." What a powerful concept, the concept that God came to earth in a flesh-and-blood body. This creative power of God was His spoken Word through which He created all things. This Word of God was manifested in the form of a human, and His name was Jesus of Nazareth. The book of Colossians says:

Who is the image of the invisible God, the first-born of every creature: For by him were all things created, that are in heaven, and that are upon earth, visible and invisible, whether thrones, or dominions, or principalities, or powers: all things were created by him, and for him: And he is before all things, and by him all things consist. (Colossians 1:15–17, King James Version)

The book of Genesis shows that on each day of creation, God spoke what happened into existence.

And God said... (Genesis 1:3)
And God said... (Genesis 1:6)
And God said... (Genesis 1:11)
And God said... (Genesis 1:14)
And God said... (Genesis 1:20)
And God said... (Genesis 1:24)
And God said... (Genesis 1:26)
And God said... (Genesis 1:29)

In the book of Genesis, God spoke everything into existence. In the book of Luke, the angel of the Lord appeared to Mary and spoke into her life according to the Modern King James. When the angel spoke to Mary, she became pregnant with the seed of the woman. The very promise of a virgin birth was fulfilled through Mary in Nazareth. Emphatically, without a doubt, Luke wrote about her question, "How can this be since I have never had sex?" The angel answered her, "The Holy Spirit will equip, protect, and prepare you, and the Highest shall overshadow you. The Word of God will conceive and bring forth the Holy child of God you will give birth to. You will call his name Jesus and he will be the Son of God" (Luke 1:28-35).

And the angel came in to her and said, Hail, one receiving grace, the Lord is with you. Blessed are you among women. And when she saw him, she was troubled at his saying, and considered what kind of greeting this might be. And the angel said to her, Do not fear, Mary, for you have found favor with God. And behold! You shall conceive in your womb and bear a son, and you shall call His name JESUS. He shall be great and shall be called the Son of the Highest. And the Lord God shall give Him the throne of His father David. And He shall reign over the house of Jacob forever, and of His kingdom there shall be no end. Then Mary said to the angel, How shall this be, since I do not know a man? And the angel answered and said to her, The Holy Spirit shall come on you, and the power of the Highest shall overshadow you. Therefore also that Holy One which will be born of you shall be called Son of God. (Luke 1:28–35, Modern King James Version)

In the book of Genesis, God told the serpent in the Garden of Eden that the seed of the woman would crush his head, according to the interpretation in the *Bible in Basic English*:

And there will be war between you and the woman and between your seed and her seed: by him will your head be crushed and by you his foot will be wounded. (Genesis 3:15) [48]

So the promise of the seed of the woman was fulfilled when Jesus of Nazareth was born. Through this seed, all members of the human race can renew their relationship with the heavenly Father. We have been separated from the things made of the Spirit through Adam's disobedience. We can be renewed to a relationship with God through His Son's obedience. One may be saying where is the proof of this? How can you say that there are more things out there than we can see? Let's look at a few examples of another world hidden from our sight in this world.

Stephen, a helper with the early believers in Jesus, was being questioned by the religious people of the time. These people were mad at him for sharing the good news of Jesus the Christ. He became so full of the presence of God that his eyes were opened and he saw past the constraints of sin into the realm of the Spirit. This is the experience described by the writer Luke in the book of Acts.

But being full of the Holy Spirit, looking up intently into Heaven, he saw the glory of God, and Jesus standing at the right hand of God. And he said, Behold, I see Heaven opened and the Son of Man standing on the right hand of God. (Acts 7:55–56, Modern King James Version)

If we look in the Old Testament in 2 Kings, we can see another instance of man being able to see into a different dimension. Elisha prayed and the Lord opened the eyes of his helper so that he could see the things of the Spirit around him.

And when the servant of the man of God had risen early, and gone forth, behold, a host compassed the city both with horses and chariots. And his servant said to him, Alas, my master! how shall we do? And he answered, Fear not: for they that are with us are more than they that are with them. And Elisha prayed, and said, LORD, I pray thee, open his eyes, that he may see. And the LORD opened the eyes of the young man; and he saw: and behold, the mountain was full of horses and chariots of fire around Elisha. (2 Kings 6:15–17, American Standard Version)

The Apostle Paul told of his experience with the Lord Jesus. How Jesus appeared to him from a different dimension and spoke to him.

And it came to pass, that as I was passing on my journey, and had come nigh to Damascus about noon, suddenly there shone from heaven a great light around me. And I fell to the ground, and heard a voice saying to me, Saul, Saul, why persecutest thou me? And I answered, Who art thou, Lord? And he said to me, I am Jesus of Nazareth, whom thou persecutest. And they that were with me saw indeed the light, and were afraid; but they heard not the voice of him that spoke to me. (Acts 22:6–9, King James Version)

Then there was the instance after Jesus was crucified and all of the disciples were in the upper room, which was locked and bolted so no one could get in or out. Jesus just appeared to the disciples and showed Himself. Then Jesus had Thomas touch Him to prove that He was really there in the room with them.

And after eight days again his disciples were within, and Thomas with them: then came Jesus, the doors being shut, and stood in the midst, and said, Peace be unto you. Then saith he to Thomas, Reach hither thy finger, and behold my hands; and reach hither thy hand, and thrust it into my side: and be not faithless, but believing. And Thomas answered and said unto him, My Lord and my God. Jesus saith unto him, Thomas, because thou hast seen me, thou hast believed: blessed are they that have not seen, and yet have believed. And many other signs truly did Jesus in the presence of his disciples, which are not written in this book: But these are written, that ye might believe that Jesus is the Christ, the Son of God; and that believing ye might have life through his name. (John 20:26–31, King James Version)

The number of times the Bible records a visitation or vision into a different dimension is great. I have mentioned a few to bring the concept home that there is more around us than what we can relate to through our senses. We can see that there is a realm all around us that we don't have access to in our flesh-and-blood bodies except by prayers through the name of Jesus.

Maybe you are not satisfied that God's provision for Adam's restoration was through the birth of Jesus of Nazareth. Let's look at the New Testament and see what other nuggets we can find that enhance the understanding of *Genesis 1-2-3*. Notice, I am not steering you away from Genesis, but bringing you back to it. If my beliefs do not fit in every way what is being expressed, than I have to rethink my beliefs, don't I?

Leaving us in this lower state would be reason to make a lot of people bitter, but the love of God never quits. God had a contingency plan. After Adam's sin, God told the serpent in Genesis 3:15 that the seed of the woman would bruise his head. In other words a woman would have a child that would renew man spiritually and place him back in a relationship with God.

And so it is written, The first man Adam was made a living soul, the last Adam was made a vivifying spirit. However, that was not first which is spiritual, but that which is natural; and afterward that which is spiritual. The first man is from the earth, earthy: the second man is the Lord from heaven. As is the earthy, such are they also that are earthy: and as is the heavenly, such are they also that are heavenly. And as we have borne the image of the earthy, we shall also bear the image of the heavenly. (1 Corinthians 15:45–49, 1833 Webster Bible) [49]

In 1 Corinthians 15:45 the Bible says the first man Adam was made a living soul; the last Adam was made a quickening spirit. First Corinthians 15:46 goes on to say that the first Adam was natural and the second Adam was spiritual. While 1 Corinthians 15:47–48 says that a natural-minded man is concerned about the earth, a spiritual-minded man is concerned about heaven.

Who was this second Adam? Notice that God was not speaking to Eve when He said the seed of the woman would bruise the serpent's head. He was talking to the serpent because the serpent was the instrument that caused Eve to disobey God. God wanted the serpent to know that through a woman God would bring forth a child who would return humanity to its proper position. All through the Old Testament, God reveals the Messiah, the Anointed, the Sent One, the Great I AM, the One Who Is and Is to Come, the Prince of Peace, the King of Kings, the Lord of Lords, the Beginning and the End, the Lamb of God, the Christ, and many more representative names for that child who was to come. The prophet Isaiah wrote in Isaiah 7:14—six hundred eighty years before this child's birth—that He would be born of a virgin. The prophet Micah wrote in Micah 5:2—seven hundred years before the child's birth—that this ruler was to be born in Bethlehem. Because of Abraham's obedience, God said in Genesis 22:16–18 that this child would be a descendant of his. This prophecy was written 1,446 years before the child was born. We know Him best as Jesus, who was brought up in Nazareth about two thousand years ago.

The story of Jesus fits in the first three chapters of Genesis like a glove. No other person who has ever walked the face of the earth can measure up to the truth of *Genesis 1-2-3*. Jesus has fulfilled the promises made to Adam and Eve in these first three chapters.

Chapter 9

God Makes Provision for This World

Looking ahead toward the fulfillment of all of the blessings that are to come to humanity in spite of the sin of Adam and Eve truly shows a God of mercy and love. As we look in the book of Genesis, we see the disobedient act and the effects of that act. Even though God created hardships for Adam and Eve because of their sin consciousness, we still see a promise from God threaded into the third chapter of Genesis.

In the first two chapters of Genesis, we see the description of the creation of the heaven and earth realm. Remember this realm is totally guided by the Spirit of God. This realm is the realm that took generations to complete. This realm is the realm where all things were created. In chapter one and chapter two of Genesis, we see all things created in perfect harmony and balance. In fact, God says, according to the Modern King James Bible:

> And God saw everything that he had made, and behold, it was very good. And the evening and the morning were the sixth day. (Genesis 1:31)

In the third chapter we see the day in which God created the earth and the heaven. This is the beginning of pain, suffering, sickness, and death. This realm was created because of Adam and Eve's disobedience in the Garden of Eden. In an instant God created the environment we now live in, because God did not want man to live forever in a sin-filled life.

And the Lord God said, Behold, [1] the man has become as one of Us, [2] to know good and evil. And now, lest he put forth his hand and [3] take also of the tree of life, and eat, and live forever, therefore God sent him out from the garden of Eden. And [4] He drove out the man. And [5] He placed cherubs at the east of the garden of Eden, and a flaming sword which turned every way, to guard the way to the tree of life. (Genesis 3:22–24, King James Version, numerals added)

I have numbered the reasons God gives for creating the environment we now see, and I have listed a little clearer explanation of these numbers below.

1. Man's character changed when he disobeyed God.
2. Man was no longer just good, but he became evil also.
3. God did not want man to eat of the Tree of Life in this condition.
4. God drove man out of the Garden of Eden.
5. God placed cherubs (angels) and a flaming sword to guard the way to the Tree of Life.

When all of the above action took place, then the realm that I call a time-based environment began. The word *east* written in Genesis 3:24 means "before time began." So you could say that everything that was before Adam's sin was in a different realm (eternity). The problem with science is it only measures things that are true to the realm that we live in. This earthly realm is the realm we reside in and relate to through our senses. The place where God created all things is not the realm in which we exist right now. If one had a time machine and could travel backwards in time, just like in the movies, one could only travel backwards for around six thousand years. The reason for this is that the realm in which we now live has only been around for a little less than six thousand years. Adam was kicked out of the Garden of Eden approximately six thousand years ago. When Adam and Eve were kicked out of the Garden of Eden, they were kicked out of eternity. How do I know this? The tree of eternal life was in the Garden of Eden, and Adam could have eaten from it forever. Therefore Adam and Eve were kicked out of the eternal realm into the earthly realm. We are living in a three-dimensional world right now, and we base all laws and measurements on this three-dimensional world. The world that existed before Adam was kicked out of the eternal realm was a multifaceted, complex dimensional world with multiple plans. The world we now live in is a world controlled and dominated by the flesh. We have been so inundated with information that makes no sense to us as far as how and why we exist. We have been fed a package of lies based on theories of the ungodly. They have concocted all kinds of ideas to hide their responsibility for their own sin-filled lives.

Here are some interesting points to think about.

1. We only use around 10 to 15 percent of our brains in this present world. I believe Adam and Eve were made in eternity using 100 percent of their brains. When sin came to humanity, man changed in character and functionality.

2. Did you know we basically use two types of mathematics? One type of mathematics we use to measure things that are small. This type of mathematics works in the molecular size and smaller. The mathematics that works in the small realm will not work in the realm we live in. Why? I believe everything was fully connected and integrated in the realm in which it was created. I believe some vital links to understanding why there are differences in mathematical measurements between small and big were lost when Adam and Eve disobeyed God.

3. Our cells in our bodies replace themselves continually. So why do we age? Why do we die?

4. If one only believes what he or she can see, one obviously would not believe in atoms, air, microwaves, radio waves, sound waves, or electricity. Therefore, one could no longer use a TV, radio, microwave oven, or light bulb. One would have to quit breathing and quit worrying about the atom bomb: it doesn't exist. All the above things receive and use a product that is beyond our seeing realm. One cannot use these things without acknowledging the possibility of God. Maybe we just need to tune in our own receivers. What do you think?

5. If all living things have a DNA pattern typical only of themselves, how can they be randomly created and what is the statistical probability of this happening accidentally for each and every life-form? Can any rationally thinking person truly believe in evolution? There is not enough measurable time for all of the life-forms to randomly happen and interact with each other without a Creator.

6. Why does the human body lose a measurable amount of weight at death? The body still has the same organs,

cells, brain matter, bones, and muscles at the instant of death. What leaves? Why does the body die?

Scientific researchers have identified the Ice Age, the Age of the Dinosaur, and other types of ages. Notice that all the ages have to be measured by the elements of the earth's decay. Carbon dating is a big argument that scientists use to prove their points all of the time. Oil and coal are more evidence that the scientific fields use to argue their case. They say these oil fields and coalfields took billions of years to produce. Recently some scientists have developed a small machine that makes little chunks of coal from plant life. It takes about two hours to form coal in this machine. The basic way it works is this: one needs some kind of organic life form, then one needs moisture, and the final thing one needs is pressure. Therefore, the coal buried deep in the earth could have been formed in hours, days, or weeks. And then they say all the different layers of the earth's surface represent different ages and changes in the earth. We can use the benefits of scientific research to help us in all kinds of situations. The use of science is beneficial for a higher quality of life and the scientific fields are ordained of God. Science can only measure the things made of what they call matter (dirt or earth). Sudden changes or calamities such as earthquakes can cause layers of the earth's surface to shift position. These surface changes cannot be factored into any time frame.

For example:

A group of investigators arrive at a crime scene and start to gather information about a recent murder. They are searching for evidence in a yellow taped off area in the middle of a grassy field. It gets too dark to work, so they get a room at the closest motel because they need sleep. They decide to finish their investigation in the morning. While they sleep, a farmer who owns the field gets his tractor out and plows the yellow taped-in area under. What are the chances of these investigators gathering more evidence from this freshly plowed field? When circumstances happen that interfere with the evidence it is hard to prove anything. (Authors story)

Around four thousand years ago there was a flood. This flood is a documented fact and archeologists have found numerous remains of sea life in all of the mountain ranges of the world. The *1889 Darby Bible* says:

And Jehovah said to Noah, Go into the ark, thou and all thy house; for thee have I seen righteous before me in this generation. Of all clean beasts thou shalt take to thee by sevens, a male and its female; but of the beasts that are not clean two, a male and its female. Also of the fowl of the heavens by sevens, male and female; to keep seed alive on the face of all the earth. For in yet seven days I will cause it to rain on the earth forty days and forty nights; and every living being which I have made will I destroy from the ground. And Noah did according to all that Jehovah had commanded him. And Noah was six hundred years old when the flood of waters was on the earth. And Noah went in, and his sons, and his wife, and his sons' wives with him, into the ark, because of the waters of the flood. Of clean beasts, and of beasts that are not clean, and of fowl, and of everything that creeps on the ground, there came two and two unto Noah into the ark, male and female, as God had commanded Noah. And it came to pass after seven days that the waters of the flood were on the earth. In the six hundredth year of Noah's life, in the second month, on the seventeenth day of the month, on that same day all <u>the fountains of the great deep were broken up</u>, and the windows of heaven were opened. (Genesis 7:1–11, underline added) [50]

Notice the underlined part of the story of Noah. "The fountains of the deep were broken up" means that all of the water under the surface of the earth bubbled up. Remember, a sphere of water was formed before the land was formed out of it. God fragmented this land when water broke from beneath the earth's surface. Have you ever seen the force of water in a flood when it rains? Can you imagine what a force of water there was coming from above and below? This flood changed the face of the earth everywhere. It would have been much worse than any farmer plowing a field.

God is reaching out to us and showing us the truth. Do you have the guts to question your own beliefs? In the end science cannot be the fulfiller of anything. Only God and God alone can give us reason to live. Life is a gift from God! Don't waste it!

All of the things made of the earth were separated from the eternal realm when Adam and Eve disobeyed God. Why? Adam and Eve had authority over all things made of the earth. All things that we see are made from the earth. There are other things that God made that we don't see. They were not under Adam's authority. In 1 Corinthians 13:12, the Bible says we "see through a glass darkly."

For now we see through a glass darkly; but then face to face: now I know in part; but then shall I know even as also I am known. (1 Corinthians 13:12, King James Version)

God put together a contingency plan, because He did not want to lose us forever. He saw value in His creation. God

155

is reaching out to this dead and dying world we live in. God is a providing heavenly Father. He desires to protect and provide for every one of us. Let's look at the first things He did for Adam and Eve.

> And Jehovah God made for Adam and for his wife coats of skins, and clothed them. (Genesis 3:21, American Standard Version)

When Adam and Eve disobeyed God in the Garden of Eden, they tried in their own way to cover their situation. They sowed fig leaves together to cover themselves because they felt inadequate. Adam and Eve were created perfect and now imperfection was birthed in their lives. They were created naked but clothed in the glory of God. Now they were naked without the presence of God. Therefore God made them a better covering then their fig leaf apparel. God took an animal and killed it. He cut the skin off of this animal and made clothes to dress Adam and Eve. These clothes were for protection from the elements. These garments were a sign to Adam and Eve that God was not going to leave them without hope. This action shows God's love and compassion even to the ones who disobey Him.

The animal had to die to give Adam and Eve clothing. I can imagine how violent this must have seemed to Adam and Eve. They had never seen death in any form before. They had only eaten from the plants and trees of the Garden of Eden before this time. But God took this animal and sacrificed its life for their benefit. God made a covering for their disobedient condition. God provided for them. God knew their needs. God had a plan to redeem their misconduct. God began to make a way. God will always make a way when there appears to be no way. Adam and Eve didn't fully understand the whole picture of what God had done. But we see a loving caring God reaching out to help them in their troubled situation.

When God killed this animal to make clothes for Adam and Eve, it had to be a bloody sight. If you are a hunter, you know what I mean. The veins that connect the skin to the rest of the body are plentiful. In fact, the largest organ of our bodies, according to science, is our skin. As God cut the skin loose from the rest of the animal's carcass, blood covered God's hands. Blood was spilled out of this animal's body for Adam and Eve's benefit. The provision that God was making for Adam and Eve became a scarlet thread of provision interwoven throughout the Scriptures written for man giving him hope. This God-ordained sacrifice was the beginning of a promise made to man called a blood covenant. This blood covenant is based on the concept that God made man for fellowship. Man separated himself from God because of his disobedient act in the Garden of Eden. Man's character changed, and God saw value in man in spite of his flawed character. Even though Adam disobeyed God in the Garden of Eden, God's desire is not to lose the fellowship of humanity. Even though humanity didn't measure up to the standards of a holy God, God would make a way for humanity to once again have fellowship with a holy God. This loving act of a sovereign God displays His character as a God full of mercy and grace continually reaching out to humanity in spite of man's fallen character.

Even though Genesis 3 doesn't present an explanation about the blood covenant, it introduces the blood covenant to humanity at this time. We see a type and shadow of God's plan for humanity. This covering by the skin of an animal is a sign of the sacrifice God is going to provide for man's condition. Types and shadows are presented throughout the Scriptures, revealing the character of God. These types and shadows are glimpses into the world the way it was originally created in the first chapter of Genesis. The world we now live in is a temporal world, not the eternal world where God resides.

> One could say Adam and his offspring were sentenced to prison like a thief goes to jail for life. But God is in the process of taking legal action to deliver Adam and his offspring from this prison. Satan is the warden of the prison and wants to keep Adam in jail forever. Not only is Satan the warden, but he is also the person who set our distant relative Adam up for the crime he committed. Adam has long ago died, but all of humanity has been born into this prison. God has not forgotten us, and He is continually bringing legal action to get all of humanity out of the devil's flesh-ruled prison. (Authors story)

God made an agreement with Adam and Eve based on the covering of clothing He gave. The animal had to die to give the skin; therefore the animal became a replacement or stand-in for Adam and Eve's disobedience. This substitute didn't replace the covering of the presence of God's glory, but it fulfilled the purpose of protection until the glory of God could be restored. Because of this replacement, there was a transfer of the skin from the animal to humanity. This transfer set up a covenant agreement in a process of time, based on what humanity should not do called the Law of God or the Ten Commandments. Notice that Adam and Eve were given one thing not to do, but Moses was given ten things not to do. Let's take a quick look at the scarlet thread of hope sewn throughout the Bible. This scarlet thread of hope is the blood covenant agreement initiated by God.

The *Bible in Basic English* says:

And without blood there is no forgiveness. (Hebrews 9:22)[51]

God initiated forgiveness when He covered Adam and Eve with the skin of this animal in the garden. In order for this forgiveness to happen, blood had to be shed. This set up the first property of the blood covenant shown in the above Scripture. This promise was a contractual agreement using blood to cover disobedience and initiate forgiveness. The blood was shed from the animal for a covering for Adam and Eve. This covering was God expressing His forgiveness for Adam and Eve's actions. This covering of the skin also shows God's desire to provide for us, even though Adam and Eve committed treason in the Garden of Eden and were kicked out of the Garden. Covering Adam and Eve with the skin of an animal shows God's desire to give unmerited favor to all of humanity.

God said, "The seed of the woman would smash the serpent's head." (Genesis 3:15) This statement shows that a woman would give birth to a person who would undo what the serpent had accomplished through Satan's influence. In other words God was going to undo what the serpent had done through a person. God gave man a promise. God gave humanity hope in a time of great despair and need. Adam and Eve had to have been at the lowest point of their existence. These words coupled with the covering of the animal skins had to feel like a warm blanket on a cold night and salve to soothe an injury. God made this blood sacrifice, provided a covering, and gave this promise. Now He waits! What is He waiting for? God is waiting for someone to act on what He said and what He did.

This person will have to be a special person. This person will have to be a person who is willing to operate according to God's promise. This person is a person who will begin to copy how God performed. Man was made in God's own image, and God was looking for someone to act on it. God was looking for that special person who was trying to reflect back to God His actions. God was looking for someone who was looking to God as his Hero. God was waiting for a person who would worship Him. God is looking for someone who wants to have fellowship with Him. This person will have to exercise a practice of believing in God. This person's motivational practice of trying to fulfill God's will in his or her own life is the end result of what God calls acting in faith.

God operates by faith, and because He operates by faith, He is looking for people who do the same. When God framed the heavens and earth, God used faith in His word to create all things. The first man that God found who would put this faith principle to work was Abel. The story is told like this in the *1833 Webster Bible*:

> And in process of time it came to pass, that Cain brought of the fruit of the ground an offering to the LORD. And Abel, he also brought of the firstlings of his flock, and of the fat thereof. And the LORD had respect to Abel, and to his offering: But to Cain and to his offering he had not respect. And Cain was very wroth, and his countenance fell. (Genesis 4:3–5) [52]

If you notice in the story above, Abel was copying what God had done for Adam and Eve when they disobeyed God in the Garden of Eden. Cain was operating out of what he had always done. Cain was following after the things the way they are, but Abel was remembering the covering God gave Adam and Eve in their sin. Abel took the first of his flock and all parts of it, even the fat, as an offering to God's promise of deliverance. If you ever try to start operating by faith in God, you will find a person who will come against

you. The person that comes against you might be your own
brother like Cain was or the person could be just a close
friend.

> And the LORD said to Cain, Why art thou wroth?
> and why is thy countenance fallen? If thou doest
> well, shalt thou not be accepted? and if thou doest
> not well, sin lieth at the door. And to thee shall be his
> desire, and thou shalt rule over him. (Genesis 4:6–7,
> 1833 Webster Bible) [53]

When God showed favoritism to Abel over Cain, it
created a deep-seated hurt with Cain. God told Cain, "Why
be angry? If you do well, I will accept you too." Cain had
a choice; he could change his own behavioral patterns, or
he could try and change Abel's. People with mixed-up ideas
make wrong decisions often. Cain was doing his best to
please himself. Abel was doing his best to please God. When
a person is a self-seeker like Cain, he or she will do whatever
it takes to maintain his or her own lifestyle. A self-seeker
is more interested in his or her own self being pleased than
anything else. If a self-seeker can't change you, he or she
will do whatever it takes to maintain status quo. The *1833
Webster Bible* also says:

> And Cain talked with Abel his brother: and it came
> to pass when they were in the field, that Cain rose
> up against Abel his brother, and slew him. And the
> LORD said to Cain, Where is Abel thy brother? And
> he said, I know not: Am I my brother's keeper? And
> he said, What hast thou done? the voice of thy broth-
> er's blood crieth to me from the ground. And now art
> thou cursed from the earth, which hath opened her
> mouth to receive thy brother's blood from thy hand;
> When thou tillest the ground, it shall not henceforth

yield to thee its strength: A fugitive and a vagabond
shalt thou be in the earth. And Cain said to the LORD,
My punishment is greater than I can bear. (Genesis
4:8–13)[54]

Cain apparently did not like the conversation he had with
his brother Abel. Cain killed Abel! The response that Cain
gave God when He inquired about Abel's whereabouts was,
"I know not: Am I my brother's keeper?" What kind of a
response is that? Cain had no remorse about having taken
Abel's life, and he lied about what had happened to Abel.
Maybe Cain couldn't see the difference in killing an animal
and Abel. Abel had the better act of worship to God and now
he was murdered because of it. The act of an animal sacrifice
gave Abel right standing with God, or you could say Abel
was made righteous. Because of his right standing in God's
eyes, Abel's righteous blood cried out from the ground when
it made contact with the earth. God cursed the earth for Cain
because of this murder, and Cain felt the punishment was too
harsh for him. Cain's love was to farm the ground and now
the ground had a curse on it. What Cain loved the most and
was good at was cursed, and Cain felt overwhelmed by this
curse. Cain didn't feel remorseful for having taken Abel's
life. He felt sorry for himself because what he loved to do
came under a curse. Cain was a self-centered, narrow-minded
religious zealot who only cared about his own beliefs and
well-being. Cain figured things out so they would be best for
him. Anyone who did not agree with him or who was against
his beliefs Cain had no problem killing. What kind of a religion is that? Does this kind of religion sound familiar? Cain
was the first terrorist!

God had found a man of faith and purpose called Abel.
Cain killed him for selfish reasons. Cain thought he would
gain something by killing Abel, but righteous Abel's blood

cried out from the ground to God. "I am not guilty! I am innocent! I have been killed for jealous reasons!"

The next key man to operate by faith was Noah. Noah so fulfilled the things of God that God called him a preacher of righteousness. The *Modern King James Version* says:

> By faith Noah, having been warned by God of things not yet seen, moved with fear, prepared an ark to the saving of his house, by which he condemned the world and became heir of the righteousness which is according to faith. (Hebrews 11:7)

Noah was warned by God about future things that were going to happen in the earth because of man's heart after the things of the flesh. Noah moved with fear! The word *fear* means Noah operated in reverential respect toward God. He listened to God. Noah obeyed God's voice and built the ark. One could say Noah acted in a positive manner and obeyed the voice of God when it was not the popular thing to do. Noah exercised his faith by building this huge boat while other people were doing their own thing. Noah, because of his obedience to God's voice, saved his wife and children from the flood to come. This action that Noah displayed day after day caused Noah to be made righteous in the eyes of God. This action was faith in what God told him to do. Why? As Noah continued to build the huge boat in obedience to God's voice, Noah condemned the people who were following after the things of the flesh-driven world man was now in. This action on Noah's part caused him to be the heir of righteousness. Noah was made to be righteous because of his willingness to be different and obey the voice of God.

This act of faith that Noah preformed in building the boat gave God the ability to make an agreement with Noah. This agreement was called a covenant. This is the first time the word *covenant* appears in the Bible. God gave a promise to man because of Noah's action. Not only did God give a promise, but He also gave a sign or a token of this covenant. We see this story in the *Modern King James Version.*

> And God spoke to Noah, and to his sons with him, saying, Behold! I, even I, establish My covenant with you, and with your seed after you; and with every living creature that is with you, of the birds, of the cattle, and of every animal of the earth with you; from all that go out from the ark, to every animal of the earth. And I will establish My covenant with you. Neither shall all flesh be cut off any more by the waters of a flood. Neither shall there any more be a flood to destroy the earth. And God said, This is the token of the covenant which I make between Me and you and every living creature with you, for everlasting generations: I set my rainbow in the cloud. And it shall be a token of a covenant between Me and the earth. And it shall be, when I bring a cloud over the earth, that the rainbow shall be seen in the cloud. And I will remember My covenant which is between Me and you and every living creature of all flesh; and the waters shall no more become a flood to destroy all flesh. And the rainbow shall be in the cloud. And I will look upon it that I may remember the everlasting covenant between God and every living creature of all flesh that is upon the earth. And God said to Noah, This is the token of the covenant which I have established between Me and all flesh that is upon the earth. (Genesis 9:8–17)

God calls this flood and the obedience of Noah to perform according to everything that God had told him to do a covenant agreement. The sign of this covenant agreement for all flesh is a rainbow. God established this covenant

agreement through Noah's obedience and Noah's willingness to perform all things that God asked him to do. One sees
this in the *Bible in Basic English.*

> By faith Noah, being moved by the fear of God, made
> ready an ark for the salvation of his family, because
> God had given him news of things which were not
> seen at the time; and through it the world was judged
> by him, and he got for his heritage the righteousness
> which is by faith. (Hebrews 11:7)[55]

Noah's obedience gave him the heritage of righteous-
ness, which is by faith. God is looking for obedience to what
He is calling you to do. Do you want God's best in your life?
Do what He wants you to do! Listen and obey; that's always
the best way. We see this written in 1 Samuel 15:22 using the
Bible in Basic English.

> And Samuel said, Has the Lord as much delight in
> offerings and burned offerings as in the doing of
> his orders? Truly, to do his pleasure is better than to
> make offerings, and to give ear to him than the fat of
> sheep. (1 Samuel 15:22, underline added)[56]

When Noah did what pleased God, his obedience was
just as powerful as Abel's sacrifice of the animal for God. For
Abel the dirt cried out, and for Noah the earth was purged. In
Abel's case righteous blood was shed. In Noah's case righteous blood was saved. Abel was slain, but Noah was deliv-
ered. Both were used of God in a mighty way, improving our
position with God. Each one took us one step closer toward
God's divine plan.
    One thing I would like to point out here. Obey God! If
you find it hard to know what to do, obey what you read
in the Bible. Pray and obey God's Word. Never sacrifice

to God in place of obeying Him. I have seen many people make sacrificial offerings to God to get God's blessing. If you are not obeying what God tells you to do, you can sacrifice all you have, but you will not have the full blessing of God flowing in your life until you OBEY GOD. People have a tendency sometimes to sacrifice instead of obeying Him. How do I know? I have done it too many times myself. If you want to be on the fast track to success, obey God. Do what you can do with what you have where you are right now. Act in faith! Follow your passion! If you keep doing what you are doing, you will keep getting what you already have gotten. The first step in making a change is prayerful listening, not speaking. The second step is doing what you know to do in your knower (gut). The third step is reminding yourself continually about what you are doing and where you are going. If you have a dream and direction from God, you will be full of passion and you will begin to talk about God's direction to others. You won't be able to stop yourself. The passion will be in you, and it will have to come out. If you still don't know what to do, follow after peace with God. He will give you direction when the right time comes. Until then, be available and put your hands to whatever there is to do for Him. Read His Word and praise Him. Ask Him to be involved in all you do. If you do all of this and walk in forgiveness, God will pour out a blessing beyond your wildest dreams. How do I know? Where do you think this book came from?

In the case of Noah, there was a sign from God to confirm a covenant agreement. This sign, the rainbow, testifies to a promise that God will not destroy the whole earth again by a flood. In the case of Abraham, we see that Abraham gives the sign of his covenant agreement. Both obeyed God. Noah received a sign signifying his obedience; Abraham gave a sign signifying his obedience.

What was the sign that Abraham gave for his obedience?

And when Abram was ninety-nine years old, the Lord appeared to Abram and said to him, I am the Almighty God! Walk before Me and be perfect. (Genesis 17:1, Literal Translation of the Holy Bible)

Here is Abram at the age of ninety-nine. Notice he isn't called Abraham yet. To most people he is past his prime. He is an old man! God tells Abram:

And I will make My covenant between Me and you, and will multiply you exceedingly. And Abram fell on his face. And God talked with him, saying, As for Me, behold! My covenant is with you, and you shall be a father of many nations. Neither shall your name any more be called Abram, but your name shall be Abraham. For I have made you a father of many nations. And I will make you exceedingly fruitful, greatly so, and I will make nations of you, and kings shall come out of you. And I will establish My covenant between Me and you and your seed after you in their generations for an everlasting covenant, to be a God to you and to your seed after you. And I will give the land to you in which you are a stranger, and to your seed after you, all the land of Canaan, for an everlasting possession. And I will be their God. (Genesis 17:2–8, Modern King James Version)

Abraham didn't say, "Where have you been, God? Fifty years ago when I was a young man, I could do these things." Abram was an old man who had seen a lot, been through a lot, and done a lot, but God placed in him the hunger and desire for more.

And God said to Abraham, And you shall keep My covenant, you and your seed after you in their generations. This is My covenant, which you shall keep, between Me and you and your seed after you. Every male child among you shall be circumcised. And you shall circumcise the flesh of your foreskin. And it shall be a token of the covenant between Me and you. And a son of eight days shall be circumcised among you, every male child in your generations; he that is born in the house, or bought with silver of any stranger who is not of your seed. He that is born in your house, and he that is bought with your silver, must be circumcised. And My covenant shall be in your flesh for an everlasting covenant. And the uncircumcised male child whose flesh of his foreskin is not circumcised, that soul shall be cut off from his people; he has broken My covenant. (Genesis 17:9–14, Modern King James Version)

The reasons I believe God made this single act that could not be undone or taken away, the sign of circumcision, is as follows.

1. This evidence of the covenant is hidden from the rest of the world.
2. It is a private thing just between God and the circumcised.
3. Only the ones closest to the circumcised know his convictions.
4. Even though the sign is hidden, the circumcised is aware of the covenant on a daily basis.
5. One has to shed blood to fulfill the agreement.
6. Scars are the evidence of the covenant agreement.
7. The benefit of the covenant is for the person circumcised.

8. The promise to Abraham was to him and his seed after him.
9. The reproductive organ for that seed was sacred.
10. The promise was to pass from generation to generation.
11. The covenant was to every child, but only the male had the sign.

These eleven things are a few of the facts of the covenant agreement. This covenant agreement is one more step toward God's divine purpose. This blood covenant agreement was for Abraham and his offspring. It was for his seed in a singular context, but the blood covenant was to be multiplied for all of his offspring and to the nations of the world. This covenant agreement signifies that the blessing of the covenant would overflow on other people beyond his own nation through his seed.

The greatest act of obedience written in the Old Testament was:

And it happened after these things that God tested Abraham, and said to him, Abraham! And he said, Behold me. And He said, Take now your son, your only one, Isaac, whom you love. And go into the land of Moriah, and offer him there for a burnt offering upon one of the mountains which I will name to you. (Genesis 22:1–2, Literal Translation of the Holy Bible)

God knew Abraham's heart! He knew that Abraham loved Isaac, and the promise was given to him and his son Isaac, but God told him to take the son of promise and offer him as a burnt offering in the land of Moriah.

And Abraham rose up early in the morning, and saddled his ass, and took two of his young men with him, and Isaac his son. And he split the wood for the burnt offering, and rose up and went to the place of which God had told him. Then on the third day, Abraham lifted up his eyes and saw the place afar off. (Genesis 22:3–4, Modern King James Version)

Abraham got up in the morning, got two young men and his son Isaac ready, cut the wood for the burnt offering, and saddled his work animal.

And Abraham said to his young men, You stay here with the ass. And I and the boy will go on to this way and worship, and come again to you. (Genesis 22:5, Modern King James Version)

Abraham left his help, two young men, with the animals and all of their provisions for their journey. He told them, "You stay here and tend to the donkey. My young son and I will go up unto the mountain and worship the Lord." Abraham's faith in God is revealed by his statement, "I and the lad will worship and come back to you." He knew what he was going to do, but he was fully persuaded that God would raise Isaac up.

And Abraham took the wood of the burnt offering, and laid it upon Isaac his son; and he took the fire in his hand, and a knife; and they went both of them together. And Isaac spake unto Abraham his father, and said, My father: and he said, Here am I, my son. And he said, Behold the fire and the wood: but where is the lamb for a burnt offering? (Genesis 22:6–7, Modern King James Version)

Notice, Abraham took the wood for the burnt offering and laid it on Isaac his son to carry, and we see Abraham carrying fire and a knife in his hands. Isaac didn't know what was happening. They must have offered animals before because Isaac said, "Where is the lamb for the burnt offering?"

And Abraham said, My son, God will provide himself a lamb for a burnt offering: so they went both of them together. (Genesis 22:8, Modern King James Version)

Abraham did not tell Isaac that he was going to be the lamb, but he told Isaac that God would provide the lamb. This had to be very troubling for Abraham as he and Isaac walked up that mountain together. When a person moves out by faith, he needs to stay in tune more than ever with what the Father is telling him. The circumstances may not look or feel right, and your mind might be telling you that you are messed up. *What a stupid idea you came up with! How could you do that?* This is where the rubber meets the road, so to speak.

And they came to the place which God had told him of; and Abraham built an altar there, and laid the wood in order, and bound Isaac his son, and laid him on the altar upon the wood. And Abraham stretched forth his hand, and took the knife to slay his son. (Genesis 22:9–10, Modern King James Version)

Abraham bound his son Isaac to the altar of wood that Isaac carried up the mountain and lifted up his knife to plunge it into his only son. This is a hard thing to think about. Can you imagine what was going through both of their minds? To get a better picture of what was happening, let's look at another Scripture.

By faith, Abraham, being tested, offered up Isaac. Yes, he who had gladly received the promises was offering up his one and only son; even he to whom it was said, "In Isaac will your seed be called;" accounting that God is able to raise up even from the dead. Figuratively speaking, he also did receive him back from the dead. (Hebrews 11:17–19, The World English Bible)

In Hebrews we see that because Abraham was convinced that if he sacrificed Isaac that God would raise him from the dead, this act of faith was accounted to him as though he had performed the act.

And the angel of the LORD called unto him out of heaven, and said, Abraham, Abraham: and he said, Here am I. And he said, Lay not thine hand upon the lad, neither do thou any thing unto him: for now I know that thou fearest God, seeing thou hast not withheld thy son, thine only son from me. (Genesis 22:11–12, King James Version)

In a fraction of a second, Abraham was able to change directions. Abraham was in tune with what God was saying. Too many times, believers keep on going in blind faith not praying or listening to the Father. We get so caught up in listening and obeying the voice of God that we lose the flexibility to change directions when He asks us to. How do I know? I have done it myself. Always, keep an open line of communication going with God, especially when you are in the process of obeying a directive from God.

And Abraham lifted up his eyes, and looked, and behold behind him a ram caught in a thicket by his horns: and Abraham went and took the ram, and offered him up for a burnt offering in the stead of his son. And Abraham called the name of that place Jehovah Jireh: as it is said to this day, In the mount of the LORD it shall be seen. And the angel of the LORD called unto Abraham out of heaven the second time, And said, By myself have I sworn, saith the LORD, for because thou hast done this thing, and hast not withheld thy son, thine only son: That in blessing I will bless thee, and in multiplying I will multiply thy seed as the stars of the heaven, and as the sand which is upon the sea shore; and thy seed shall possess the gate of his enemies; And in thy seed shall all the nations of the earth be blessed; because thou hast obeyed my voice. (Genesis 22:13–18, King James Version)

Notice, God blessed Abraham because he obeyed His voice, not because he took Isaac to be sacrificed. Do you think God would have been able to bless Abraham and his seed if he had just plunged his knife into his son? No, he would not have blessed Abraham at all. Abraham believed God to the fullest, and because he did this act, Abraham's obedience set the stage for God to send His own Son to be a sacrifice for all the nations of the world on the wooden structure called the cross.

For as in Adam all die, even so in Christ all will be made alive. (1 Corinthians 15:22, Modern King James Version)

Death came into the world because of Adam; eternal life will come through the Anointed one who is the Christ.

For what does the Scripture say? "Abraham believed God, and it was counted to him for righteousness." (Romans 4:3, Modern King James Version)

Did doubt try to come to him? I am sure doubt tried to come, but Abraham was fully persuaded. Abraham didn't concentrate on any doubts that came, nor did he get caught up in what was going on in the world around him. Abraham directed his life to believe and obey God.

He did not stagger at the promise of God through unbelief, but was strong in faith, giving glory to God, and being fully persuaded that what God had promised, He was also able to perform. And therefore it was imputed to him for righteousness. (Romans 4:20–22, Modern King James Version)

I am not going to get into all of the different men and women of faith written about in the Bible, but I am going to bring the key people to your attention. These people are necessary to understanding all of Genesis 1-2-3 as it relates to us today.

Moses is the next key man of God. God used Moses because he was a man of faith who would obey His voice. God gave Moses the laws of God; we call these the Ten Commandments. These Ten Commandments are rules to follow to be called righteous with God. Moses had to follow the blood covenant of circumcision God made with Abraham.

(For the LORD thy God is a merciful God;) he will not forsake thee, neither destroy thee, nor forget the covenant of thy fathers which he sware unto them. For ask now of the days that are past, which were before thee, since the day that God created man upon the earth, and ask from the one side[7097] of heaven unto the other, whether there hath been any such thing as this great thing is, or hath been heard like it? (Deuteronomy 4:31–32, King James Version w/one Strong's Number)

In the above Scriptures God was making a statement to Moses in Deuteronomy 4:31, reminding him of the burning bush experience he had.

1. God is merciful.
2. God will not forsake you.
3. God will not destroy you.
4. God will not forget the blood covenant.

In Deuteronomy 4:32 we see a contrast of the days past and the days present. We see the statement, "one side of heaven unto the other." The words *one side* mean, according to *Strong's Exhaustive Concordance*:

7097 qatseh kaw-tseh'
or (negative only) qetseh kay'-tseh; from 7096; an extremity (used in a great variety of applications and idioms; compare 7093): — X after, border, brim, brink, edge, end, (in-)finite, frontier, outmost coast, quarter, shore, (out-)side, X some, ut(-ter-)most (part). [57]

This word *side* means "a border, brim, brink, or edge." This word is showing a separation of man from the realm of the heaven and earth realm in which Adam and Eve were created to the earthy realm Adam and Eve were driven to because of their disobedience to God. In the Holy of Holies, the cherubim on the mercy seat represent this border, the brink of separation from one realm to the other. You could say these cherubim represent the door or the way to the eternal life Adam had before he was kicked out of heaven.

Moses was the person God used to bring the Jewish nation out of Egypt. In the process of delivering the Jewish nation out of Egypt, God instituted the Passover Lamb. This lamb became the sacrifice for the firstborn of the entire Hebrew nation. The Jewish nation to this day celebrates the Passover, which commemorates the day of deliverance out of Egypt. The Jewish people put blood over their doorposts, and the death angel passed over the Hebrew nation, even though the firstborn of every other living thing in Egypt died. The Jewish people were instructed to roast this lamb and eat it. Any remains that were left were to be burned the next morning.

One could write much about how God used Moses to deliver the Jewish nation out of Egypt. This book is about Genesis 1–3, therefore I will focus on the important part of the things Moses did pertaining to these three chapters. Moses is known to be the deliverer of Israel. No person was used in a greater way than Moses was used for the tribes of Israel in the Old Testament times. Most of the Jewish holidays have their origin during the era of the leadership of Moses. Moses is one of the most revered prophets in the Jewish belief. The most important thing that Moses did that relates to Genesis 1–3 is that he built the first temple of God. He built the temple according to God's specifications. Everything he placed in the temple had a purpose. This temple was built to be mobile. It was built to be flexible. It was built to go with the people of God. It was built to be a place of ready access. This tabernacle was a movable tent designed to go with the people of God as they lived their daily lives. Everywhere the Hebrews went; the temple of God was the visible tangible evidence of an all-powerful God involved in their lives.

It wasn't until Solomon built the temple in Jerusalem that the temple was made as a stationary place of worship.

The Babylonian armies destroyed Solomon's temple. Then Nehemiah started to rebuild the temple 538 years before Jesus was born. It wasn't completed until 516 years before the birth of Jesus. Seventy years after the death, burial, and resurrection of Jesus, the temple of God was destroyed and has never been rebuilt to this day.

Chapter 10

Jesus Is the Anointed One, Christ

W e see God working to restore all of humanity. God is always looking for people of faith, people with the right heart, and people that are reaching out to know Him more. All through the Bible we see people with that desire. These people are a called people who want more of God in their lives, with a desire for God's purpose for this world to be shown through their lives. We looked at Abel, Noah, Abraham, and Moses. These men were key players in the movement of God to a lost and dying world. Each one had purpose of heart and a conviction to fulfill God's purpose in their lives. This God of mercy and grace is continually reaching out to a disobedient world, looking for that person of God who is willing to lay his or her life down for a higher cause. God is looking for the person who will help Him fulfill His divine purpose. Someone who will obey God's voice and do what He tells them to do. These people of God have come from all walks of life. They have done radical works for God in desperate times. Their ability to hear God's voice when the masses were going the wrong way changed the future of men and women forever. The Bible is packed full of people who yielded their lives to God. The Bible is a testimony of people's lives chasing after God. Some people

in the Bible obey the voice of God and some follow after
the things of the flesh. As we see stories written of men in
the Bible, it draws me back to the promise of God written in
Genesis 3:24. Let us look at this verse written in the Modern
King James Version.

> And He drove out the man. And He placed cherubs at
> the east of the Garden of Eden, and a flaming sword
> which turned every way, to guard the way to the tree
> of life. (Genesis 3:24, Modern King James Version)

God drove out the man, but God did not stop there. This
verse is a verse that no man can argue about. It stands alone
as a beacon of light in a sea of despair. It is the final statement of fact in the creation of this world, as we know it.
From this point on, the Bible changes from the creation of
the heaven and earth realm to dealing with us in the earth
and heaven realm. We see in this verse a separation. We see
a breaking apart. We see a change of relationship. We see a
blocking of the way to the Tree of Life. We see angels sent to
guard the entrance to the Tree of Life. Not only that, but we
see a flaming sword. This sword is continually in motion. It
is always moving. What does all of this mean?

Genesis 4 begins the history of this earth- and heaven-
driven realm we now see. Remember earth represents the
things of the flesh and heaven represents the things of the
spirit. We can all look back in history to this time. If we're
alive in this world, this verse pertains to us. No matter what
we believe, this verse is the key to the truth for this world.
This verse stands alone as a pillar of truth. This verse sepa-
rates fact from fiction. This verse shows you where your
heart is. This verse strips away the lies of the religious and
bares the soul of the ungodly. This verse magnifies the truth
greater than the Hubble Space Telescope reveals the mystery
of the universe. Genesis 3:24 is like a lawyer's final state-

ment in the court of law. This verse stands alone in a sea of turbulent waters. What does Genesis 3:24 mean? This verse says these things.

1. There is a Tree of Life.
2. There is a way to the Tree of Life.
3. Two things guard this way to the Tree of Life.
   A. Cherubs (angels)
   B. A flaming sword that is continually moving.

Different people have looked for the Tree of Life, or the fountain of youth. They will not find it in this world we live in, because it is separated from this world. The Tree of Life does exist in the origin of Adam's home. This realm we have no right to because of our disobedient, sin-filled nature caused by Adam and Eve in the Garden of Eden. God created this separation for a purpose. This purpose was the divine plan of God from the foundations of the earth. What is this purpose?

The fulfillment of the divine purpose of God written about in the first three chapters of Genesis can only be fulfilled by one person. That person is Jesus of Nazareth who is the Anointed One, the Messiah, or the Christ. No other person can fulfill Genesis chapters one, two, and three. There is no man before or after Jesus who can measure up to the Holy Word of God written in Hebrew thousands of years ago. If one knows the first three chapters of Genesis and is honest with oneself, Jesus stands alone as the only possible Messiah. Mohammad, Allah, Buddha, the Pope, the Dalai Lama, or any other person cannot measure up to the truth of these three chapters. One man, Jesus, stands alone as a beacon of light to a darkened world. I dare you to take your belief and prove any other person to be the Messiah. Take your belief and show me how it fits in chapters one, two, and three of the holy book of Genesis. I can take manuscripts written thousands of years ago and prove that Jesus is the only answer to chapters 1–3 of Genesis. Who can you find? One cannot dispute these truths unless one is totally ignorant or blinded by a false religion or belief. Do not let assumption and false teaching lead you into eternal separation from the Almighty God. God loves you! He sent His Son for you! Obey God! Obey God's Word!

> And He drove out the man. And He placed cherubs at the east of the garden of Eden, and a flaming sword which turned every way, to guard the way to the tree of life. (Genesis 3:24, Modern King James Version)

The last verse of Genesis chapter three reveals a startling truth hidden from man. This truth is when Moses was instructed to build the temple of God in the form of a tent in the wilderness. These things were within the inner tent called the Holy of Holies according to the Modern King James Bible.

> And after the second veil was a tabernacle which is called the Holy of Holies, having a golden altar of incense, and the ark of the covenant overlaid all around with gold, in which was the golden pot that had manna, and Aaron's rod that budded, and the tablets of the covenant. And over it were the cherubs of glory overshadowing the mercy-seat (about which we cannot now speak piece by piece.) (Hebrews 9:3–5, Modern King James Version)

The Holy of Holies is where God would show His presence. There was a pillar of cloud by day and a pillar of fire by night. When this pillar of cloud would start to move, the people would pull up camp and follow the cloud. In the wilderness God instructed Moses to build a tabernacle. The second tent inside of the first tent was called the Holy of Holies where these things where located:

1. Golden altar of incense.
2. Ark of the Covenant overlaid with gold.
    A. Golden pot with manna.
    B. Aaron's rod that budded.
    C. Tablets of the covenant.
3. The cherubs of glory standing over the mercy seat.

The golden altar of incense represents the prayers of the people who believe. They are the sweet-smelling savor to the nostrils of a holy God (Revelations 5:8). These prayers have praised the Creator of heaven and earth. They have worshiped the Holy One. In Him, by Him, and through Him do they have their hope fixed on Him! Their prayers have gone up into the presence of the Almighty God.

The Ark of the Covenant is the vessel of hope containing the three-fold message of God to His people. The golden pot of manna represents the supernatural provision of God for His people. Aaron's rod that budded represents the miracle-working power of God. And the tablets of the covenant of God are the Law of God or the rules to fulfill the covenant of God.

This Ark of the Covenant could be called a vessel of hope to a lost and dying world. Who can measure up to the law of God? The Ark of the Covenant was covered by the mercy seat showing that only by the mercy of God can any man receive the fullness of the covenant. Except for the mercy of God, can any man attain the blessing of God?

The last things inside of the Holy of Holies are the cherubs of glory. When the high priest went into the Holy of Holies once a year for the sins of the people, he saw the cherubs. These were two angels crafted of wood and overlaid with gold. The high priest would once a year enter into this holy place to give an offering for all of the people. The high priest would go into the Holy of Holies with blood for a covering of the people's sin. While he was sprinkling the interior of the Holy of Holies, he would look at these cherubs of glory. The thoughts that would pass through his head were the disobedience of all of man. This blood offering was atonement for the disobedience of all of humanity. As God would cause him to think about the sins of the people, he would reflect back to Adam and his fall from the Garden of Eden. The high priest would see the cherubs of glory in the Holy of Holies and reflect that the way to the tree of eternal life is through the cherubs of glory. The high priest would see a representation of what Adam lost. The high priest would see a representation of the way back to the entrance of a different dimension—the Garden of Eden. The high priest saw the representation of the way to eternal life Adam had lost. He would see the cherubs and reflect back to Genesis 3:24. The way to eternal life is through the cherubs. He could not enter into eternal life, but he could make an offering for the disobedience of humanity. The high priest would see with his natural eyes a representation of what Adam lost. He would wonder when the way to the life Adam had before he disobeyed God would be restored according to God's divine plan. As he was inside of the Holy of Holies sprinkling blood over all of the interior parts, he was thinking what blood could be used to open the way through the cherubim to the Tree of Life forever?

Jesus of Nazareth, who is called the Christ, opened the way through the cherubs about two thousand years ago. When Jesus was crucified just outside of Jerusalem on a tree, He became the way or the fruit of the Tree of Life. His blood was spilled once to remove the disobedience of Adam and all of our transgressions once and for all. The high priest of Israel no longer enters into the Holy of Holies because Jesus of Nazareth has fulfilled God's divine plan. Jesus said in the Modern King James Bible:

> Jesus said to him, I am the Way, the Truth, and the Life; no one comes to the Father but by Me. (John 14:6, Modern King James Version)

Please read the whole chapter of John 14. It shows that they were talking about eternal life when Jesus made this statement to His disciples.

We see according to two witnesses that the temple veil—separating the Holy of Holies—was torn from top to bottom. This veil was four inches thick according to tradition. It was ripped apart for one purpose: to show that the way to God is opened through the cherubs by the blood of Jesus. Jesus was without sin, and He took our sin in His body and nailed it to the cross (the altar).

> And, behold, the veil of the temple was rent in twain from the top to the bottom; and the earth did quake, and the rocks rent; (Matthew 27:51, Modern King James Version)
>
> And the veil of the temple was rent in twain from the top to the bottom. (Mark 15:38, Modern King James Version)
>
> And it was about the sixth hour, and there was a darkness over all the earth until the ninth hour. And the sun was darkened, and the veil of the temple was rent in the midst. (Luke 23:44–45, Modern King James Version)

Notice that Matthew and Mark said the veil was rent or torn from the top to the bottom. These two witnesses give testimony by describing that the veil was torn from the top to the bottom. Luke on the other hand gives a description of the time in which it was torn. Luke says that in the sixth hour it became very dark. This darkness lasted until the ninth hour. Luke said half the way through this dark period, the veil was torn in two. So Matthew and Mark give a description of the veil begin torn from top to bottom, and Luke gives us the time of day the veil was torn in two between the sixth and ninth hours or at the seventh and one half hour. Matthew and Mark both tell of the darkness from the sixth hour to the ninth hour.

> Now from the sixth hour there was darkness over all the land unto the ninth hour. (Matthew 27:45, Modern King James Version)
> And when the sixth hour was come, there was darkness over the whole land until the ninth hour. (Mark 15:33, Modern King James Version)

Only Luke gives a description of when the veil was torn from the top to the bottom in the temple of God. This lets us know that Luke was either in the temple during the crucifixion of Jesus or had a good relationship with those who were in the temple. Luke was most likely the highest educated of the three, because he was a doctor. Because of this position in life, he may have come into contact with various classes of people, and he might have had some schooling with other people in different professional fields. Some of his own teachers and mentors were probably affiliated with the workers in the temple. We need to understand that the hub of existence of Luke's age revolved around the temple of God. This is probably why Luke knew the precise time that the veil was torn.

This veil was not just a piece of material like a sheet of a bed. Nor was it a piece of material like a quilt, but it was about four inches thick. John Gill's *Exposition of the Entire Bible* describes the strength of this veil.

Exodus 26:31 - And thou shalt make a vail, . . . The use of this, as follows, was to divide the holy place from the most holy place in the tabernacle; it has its name from hardness, it being very stiff and strong, for it was made of thread six times doubled, and was four fingers thick, as the Jewish writers say. [58]

Now we know this veil was about four inches thick; it was made with a thread that was six times doubled, and it was torn in two from the top to the bottom during the seventh and one-half hour. But as we look further into the making of this veil, we also see that it was very colorful.

And you shall make a veil of blue, and purple, and scarlet, and fine twined bleached linen of embroidered work. (Exodus 26:31, Modern King James Version)

These colors and the use of linen show a sign of royalty, wealth, and abundance. The veil also represents the flesh of Jesus.

By a new and living way, which he hath consecrated for us, through the veil, that is to say, his flesh; (Hebrews 10:20, Modern King James Version, underline added)

So we see according to the Scriptures that the veil represents Jesus' flesh. Let's think on this a little bit. We know the veil was torn from top to bottom. Jesus' flesh was torn on Calvary's cross. We also see in the colors of the veil in Jesus' blood. Blue is the color of the blood as it flows through Jesus' body. Purple is the color of the blood of Jesus through his skin as Jesus is beaten and bruises form in His flesh. And scarlet is the color of His blood as it flows from His flesh.

The colors of the veil not only are a sign of royalty, but they are a revelation of the body of Christ hanging on the cross of Calvary.

> And the Word was made flesh, and dwelt among us, (and we beheld his glory, the glory as of the only begotten of the Father,) full of grace and truth. (John 1:14, King James Version)

We see that the Word of God was made flesh. So now we see that the fleshly body of Jesus was the Word of God in a bodily form.

> In the beginning was the Word, and the Word was with God, and the Word was God. The same was in the beginning with God. All things were made by him; and without him was not any thing made that was made. (John 1:1–3, King James Version)

According to John's Gospel, Jesus was the manifest presence of God in a fleshly body. This total purpose is encapsulated in the word *incarnate*. We see that the Word of God was God Himself, the Creator of all things.

The only way anyone could enter this inner sanctuary of God called the Holy of Holies was through the veil with the blood of the Lamb as atonement for the sin of the people.

The veil represents Jesus' flesh. The author of Hebrews explains the full impact of what Jesus did on the cross of Calvary. The Modern King James Bible says:

> "This is the covenant that I will make with them after those days, says the Lord; I will put My Laws into their hearts, and in their minds I will write them," also He adds, "their sins and their iniquities I will remember no more." Now where remission of these is,

there is no more offering for sin. Therefore, brothers, having boldness to enter into the Holy of Holies by the blood of Jesus, by a new and living way which He has consecrated for us through the veil, that is to say, His flesh; and having a High Priest over the house of God, let us draw near with a true heart in full assurance of faith, having our hearts sprinkled from an evil conscience and our bodies having been washed with pure water. Let us hold fast the profession of our faith without wavering (for He is faithful who promised), (Hebrews 10:16–23, Modern King James Version, underline added)

So we can see that the fulfillment of God's divine plan is coming to completion. We, the ones who believe in Jesus the Christ, have the truth for all of humanity. We are the church, the body of believers in Jesus. Our covenant was cut two thousand years ago on Calvary's cross. Jesus fulfilled the covenants of Noah and Abraham, and fulfilled the Law of Moses. Because of Jesus, we have right standing with the Almighty God. Jesus has made us righteous in God's eyes. Jesus is the seed of the woman that smashed the serpent's head (Genesis 3:15). Jesus is the promise given to Adam and Eve by God for all of humanity.

For since by man came death, by man came also the resurrection of the dead. For as in Adam all die, even so in Christ shall all be made alive. (1 Corinthians 15:21–22, 1833 Webster Bible) [59]

In 1 Corinthians the Bible says that all of mankind is in a dead and dying world because of Adam's disobedience. The Bible also states that in the Christ shall all have the ability to be alive again. In other words through Jesus shall all restoration come for eternal life.

But someone will say, How are the dead raised up, and with what body do they come? Foolish one! What you sow is not made alive unless it dies. And what you sow, you do not sow the body that *is* going to be, but a bare grain (perhaps of wheat or of some of the rest). And God gives it a body as it has pleased Him, and to each of the seeds its own body. All flesh *is* not the same flesh; but one *kind of* flesh of men, and another flesh of beasts, and another of fish, and another of birds. *There are* also heavenly bodies and earthly bodies. But the glory of the heavenly *is* truly different, and that of the earthly different; one glory of *the* sun, and another glory of *the* moon, and another glory of *the* stars; for *one* star differs from *another* star in glory So also the resurrection of the dead. It is sown in corruption, it is raised in incorruption; it is sown in dishonor, it is raised in glory; it is sown in weakness, it is raised in power; it is sown a natural body, it is raised a spiritual body. There is a natural body, and there is a spiritual body. And so it is written, "The first man, Adam, became a living soul," the last Adam was a life-giving Spirit. (1 Corinthians 15:35–45, Modern King James Version)

Adam partook of the fruit of the wood in disobedience in the Garden of Eden but Jesus obeyed God in the Garden of Gethsemane and went to the cross (wood) for all of us. "O My Father, if it is possible, let this cup pass from Me. Yet not as I will, but as You will" (Mathew 26:39). Jesus began the process of undoing what the natural man Adam had done by eating of the tree of good and evil. Jesus became the life-giving spiritual man when he laid down His fleshy desire and obeyed God.

But not the spiritual first, but the natural; afterward the spiritual. The first man *was* out of earth, earthy; the second Man *was* the Lord from Heaven. (1 Corinthians 15:46–47, Modern King James Version)

Another statement that was made in Genesis 3:24 is there was a flaming sword that turns every way to guard the way of the Tree of Life.

And He drove out the man. And He placed cherubs at the east of the garden of Eden, and <u>a flaming sword which turned every way, to guard the way</u> to the tree of life. (Genesis 3:24, Modern King James Version, underline added)

This flaming sword is the Word of God. *Flaming* means it is ablaze. The fact that the sword is continually turning means it is alive and moving. This flaming sword is doing something. It is guarding the way to the Tree of Life. The word *guard* means according to the *Strong's Hebrew and Greek Dictionaries.*

8104 shamar shaw-mar'
a primitive root; properly, to hedge about (as with thorns), i.e. guard; generally, to protect, attend to, etc.:—beward, be circumspect, take heed (to self), keep(-er, self), mark, look narrowly, observe, preserve, regard, reserve, save (self), sure, (that lay) wait (for), watch(-man). [60]

So this word *guard* means "to protect, preserve, reserve, save, and keep" the way to the truth of the Tree of Life. According to the Modern King James Bible, we see that the sword of the Spirit is the Word of God.

And the sword of the Spirit, which is the Word of God
. . . (Ephesians 6:17, Modern King James Version)

In Hebrews we see that the Word of God is alive and is
sharper than the Roman fighting sword.

For the Word of God is living and powerful and
sharper than any two-edged sword, piercing even to
the dividing apart of soul and spirit, and of the joints
and marrow, and is a discerner of the thoughts and
intents of the heart. (Hebrews 4:12, Modern King
James Version)

We see that this sword can cut to the mind and heart of
man and can see his intent for life. This sword in Genesis
3:24 is guarding the way and the truth to eternal life. This
sword cuts away the flesh and shows the true purpose of
God. This sword reveals the truth of your relationship with
God. This sword reveals the true motive of your heart and
opens it so that all may see.

So we see in Genesis 3:24 a flaming sword that turns
every direction. This flaming sword is the Word of God.
The Word of God is ablaze or on fire. The Word of God is
hot with compassion to all of humanity. The Word of God
is alive and quick and more powerful than any two-edged
sword (Hebrews 4:12). The Word of God is constantly in
motion moving and turning every direction to every person.
The Word of God is constantly opening the fleshly body,
stripping away the flesh, and baring the hidden heart condition of man. The Word of God is continually convicting our
consciences and showing us the truth. The Bible is the Word
of God to this dead and dying three-dimensional flesh-driven
world we live in called earth. It is not only protecting the way
to the Tree of Life in the Garden of Eden, but it is showing

the way to eternal life through Jesus the Christ our Lord and Savior.

For Christ has not entered into the Holy of Holies made with hands, which are the figures of the true, but into Heaven itself, now to appear in the presence of God for us. Nor yet that He should offer Himself often, even as the high priest enters into the Holy of Holies every year with the blood of others (for then He must have suffered often since the foundation of the world), *but now once* in the end of the world *He has appeared to put away sin by the sacrifice of Himself.* And as it is appointed to men once to die, but after this, the judgment, so Christ was once offered to bear the sins of many. And to those who look for Him He shall appear the second time without sin to salvation. (Hebrews 9: 24-28, Modern King James Version, Italic, and under line added)

We see the undeniable all-consuming truth of Genesis 1–3. My heart's cry is that all will come to know Jesus the Christ. It is my desire to see all who read this come to know God through the precious blood of Jesus.

Please read this prayer out loud with your mouth, so that the words will flow out of your lips and free your heart from the bondage of sin.

Heavenly Father, I see the truth. I know the truth. I accept the truth. Right now in my life, I say with my mouth and believe with all of my heart that Jesus shed His blood for me. That Jesus died on the cross for me. That Jesus fulfilled God's divine plan for my life. Jesus took my sin on Calvary's cross. I accept what Jesus has done for me and accept Jesus as my Lord and Savior from this day forward. I thank You, Lord, that I am headed for eternal life. That from this day forward I am heaven bound. I say all of this under the power and authority of Jesus Christ my Lord and Savior. Amen!

Now I leave you with one portion of the Scriptures that has helped me to see the truth of who Jesus really was compared to every other religious person.

Beloved, do not believe every spirit, but try the spirits to see if they are of God, because many false prophets have gone out into the world. By this you know the Spirit of God: every spirit that confesses that Jesus Christ has come in the flesh is of God. (1 John 4:1–2, Modern King James Version)

This Scripture was written more than 1,900 years ago. It says that every spirit that confesses that Jesus has come in the flesh is of God. Notice that this Scripture is talking about the spirit part of man. This Scripture is talking about a confession from the spirit of man. Not just man saying Jesus has come in the flesh. Different religions believe Jesus came in the flesh and say that they know He did. The word *confession* means more than just saying words. *Confession* means "from a deep heartfelt agreement from the core of the center of your being." Not just saying words. Let's look at Romans 10:9–10 in the King James Bible.

That if thou shalt confess with thy mouth the Lord Jesus, and shalt believe in thy heart that God hath raised him from the dead, thou shalt be saved. For with the heart man believeth to righteousness; and with the mouth confession is made to salvation. (Romans 10:9–10)

The heart of man is the same as saying the spirit of man. If you notice it says to confess with your mouth and believe with all of your heart that God raised Jesus from the dead. The heart or spirit of man has become righteous because with your belief you have confessed with your mouth salvation.

John points out in the epistle of 1John that God is looking at the spirit of man. The below Scriptures are written in such away to be directed to the spirit portion of man. John is talking about the spirit of man the real you not the outer shell of your body but the motivating force within your body.

> And <u>every spirit that does not confess</u> that Jesus Christ has come in the flesh <u>is not of God</u>. And this is the antichrist you heard is coming, and even now is already in the world. You are of God, little children, and you have overcome them, because He who is in you is greater than he who is in the world. They are of the world, therefore they speak of the world, and the world hears them. We are of God. He who knows God hears us. *<u>The one who is not of God does not hear us</u>.* **From this we know the spirit of truth and the spirit of error.** (1 John 4:3–6, Modern King James Version, emphasis and underline added)

The 1 John 4:3–6 says there is a spirit of truth and there is a spirit of error. This is a warning John wrote more than 1,800 years ago. He wrote in 1 John 4:3, according to the Modern King James Bible, that every spirit that does not confess that Jesus is the Christ is of the spirit of error. Jesus is the Anointed One or the Messiah. Therefore all books, all religions, and all beliefs that have come after the writing of the Scripture and have tried to redirect seekers away from Jesus are not of God. All of these people are of the antichrist. The Bible says it plainly: you are not of God if you don't accept what Jesus did for you on Calvary's cross. These Scriptures were written more than 1,800 years ago. They are God's promise to us. Do not let anybody add to or take away from these Holy Scriptures. Do not be so foolish as to let someone write a new document that is a better way. Notice, they will always quote the Bible. The Bible never quotes them. Just like the devil when he tempted Jesus. The devil quoted the Scriptures to tempt Jesus. Jesus answered back with the Scriptures to answer this temptation. Jesus did not change God's Scriptures nor did He write new ones. Jesus fulfilled God's promises to all of humanity. The devil tried to twist or change the Scripture for an earthly purpose. Jesus remained focused on the heavenly purpose.

Muhammad's earliest teachings emphasized his belief in one transcendent but personal God, the Last Judgment, and social and economic justice. God, he asserted, had sent prophets to other nations throughout history, but, having failed to reform, those nations had been destroyed. Muhammad proclaimed his own message, the Qur'an, to be the last revealed Book and himself to be the last of the prophets, consummating and superseding the earlier ones. [61][underline added]

Islam is of the antichrist because it was written long after the Scriptures were written. The book of John was written less than fifty years after Jesus arose from the dead. Muhammad's Qur'an or Koran was written more than six hundred years after John wrote 1 John 4:3–6. John wrote this Scripture to keep people from listening to the spirit of error.

Muhammad (570?–632), founder of Islam, whose prophetic teachings, encompassing political and social as well as religious principles, became the basis of Islamic civilization and have had a vast influence on world history. Muhammad was born in Mecca. He belonged to the clan of Hashim, a poor but respected branch of the prestigious and influential tribe of Quraysh. His father died before he was born, and after his mother's death when he was six, he was brought up by his uncle Abu Talib. Pensive and with-drawn in temperament, he displayed an acute moral sensitivity at an early age, and he was known as al-Amin ("the trusted one"). Like his fellow tribesmen, he became a trader and made several journeys to Syria, where he may have met and conversed with Christians. He then began to manage the business of a rich widow, Khadija; she was greatly impressed by both his honesty and ability, and she shortly offered him marriage, which he accepted at the age of 25. [62]

As you can see, Muhammad took the focus off of Jesus and refocused the direction of belief to his own thoughts and writings by saying that the Jewish nation would not listen to God, so God sent Muhammad to direct the world. Muhammad's teachings do not bring you to Jesus but draw you away by twisting the truth for an earthy purpose. You may get angry and want to kill me for this, but I love you just like Jesus did when He went to the cross for you and me. Jesus is alive and able to save you to the uttermost. Cain didn't want to obey God, so he killed righteous Abel. You may not want to obey the truth, but if you kill me, my blood will cry out to the Lord.

Open their eyes Lord to the truth that Jesus is the way the truth and the life. Nobody comes to the Father but by the way-maker Jesus of Nazareth who is the Christ (Anointed One).

Some beliefs or religions try to say that man will have a special place for fulfilling a special cause in this earth. No man is justified in this world by any act. No one can kill a person and justify it because of a religious belief. The Islamic belief says that they are going to rule the world. The world is the flesh! Never be taught in a religion to bring a purpose for the flesh in this world. To teach someone they will have a number of virgins in the afterlife is contrary to the Scriptures. The Scriptures say in the Modern King James Bible that there is no sex in the afterlife.

Then came to him certain of the Sadducees (who deny that there is any resurrection) and they asked him, Saying, Master, Moses wrote to us, If any man's brother should die, having a wife, and he should die without children, that his brother should take his wife, and raise up seed to his brother. There were therefore seven brothers: and the first took a wife, and died without children. And the second took her for a wife, and he died childless. And the third took her; and in like manner the seven also: And they left no children, and died. Last of all the woman died also. Therefore in the resurrection, whose wife of them is she? for seven had her to wife. And Jesus answering, said to them, The children of this world marry, and are given in marriage: **But they who shall be accounted worthy to obtain that world, and the resurrection from the dead, neither marry, nor are given in marriage. Neither can they die any more: for they are equal to the angels; and are the children of God, being the children of the resurrection.** (Luke 20:27–36, emphasis added)

Notice the New Testament that was written more than 1,800 years ago says there will be no sexual activity in the eternal realm. We will be equal to the angels, and we will be the children of God. Any teaching that is contrary to the Holy Bible is from the father of all lies. All terrorists will be very disappointed when they see the other side.

Jesus said two things I want to leave with you.

And he said unto them, Go ye into all the world, and preach the gospel to every creature. He that believeth and is baptized shall be saved; but he that believeth not shall be damned. (Mark 16:15–16, Modern King James Version)
I am the door. If anyone enters in by Me, he shall be saved and shall go in and out and find pasture. The thief does not come except to steal and to kill and to destroy. I have come so that they might have life, and that they might have it more abundantly. (John 10:9-10, Modern King James Version)

My prayer is that this book will be printed in every language and spread throughout every continent and island in this fallen world we all live in called earth. I pray that this message will impact the world like never before, that this message sets the masses free from the bondages of false religions. Revival, I ask for revival like this world has never seen before. I believe this book is a type of forerunner to usher in the return of Jesus. I believe people's eyes will be opened to the truth and that truth will set them free. You may not feel secure enough to preach, but you can give this book away.

But you shall receive power, the Holy Spirit coming upon you. And you shall be witnesses to Me both in Jerusalem and in all Judea, and in Samaria, and to the end of the earth. And saying these things, as they watched, He was taken up. And a cloud received Him out of their sight. And while they were looking intently into the heaven, He having gone, even behold, two men in white clothing stood beside them, who also said, Men of Galilee, why do you stand gazing up into the heaven? This same Jesus who is taken up from you into Heaven, will come in the way you have seen Him going into Heaven. (Act 1:8–11, Modern King James Version)

Get ready! Jesus is coming back!

Notes

In addition to the references below, I would highly recommend that anyone interested in an abundance of Bible resources go online to e-sword.com. Rick Meyers has done a wonderful job of putting together the best downloadable software to research any Bible question for free. Thank you, Rick. From the bottom of my heart, I thank you and pray that God richly blesses you now and for all eternity.

1 "Evolution," *Microsoft Encarta Encyclopedia 2000.* © 1993–1999 Microsoft Corporation. All rights reserved.
2 "Bible," *Microsoft Encarta Encyclopedia 2000.* © 1993– 1999 Microsoft Corporation. All rights reserved.
3 "Strong's Hebrew and Greek Dictionaries," *e-Sword Version 7.8.5* © 2000-2007 Rick Meyers. All rights reserved.
4 "Strong's Hebrew and Greek Dictionaries," *e-Sword Version 7.8.5* © 2000-2007 Rick Meyers. All rights reserved.
5 "Strong's Hebrew and Greek Dictionaries," *e-Sword Version 7.8.5* © 2000-2007 Rick Meyers. All rights reserved.
6 "1898 Young's Literal Translation," *e-Sword Version 7.8.5* © 2000-2007 Rick Meyers. All rights reserved.

7 "Strong's Hebrew and Greek Dictionaries," *e-Sword Version 7.8.5* © 2000-2007 Rick Meyers. All rights reserved.

8 "Strong's Hebrew and Greek Dictionaries," *e-Sword Version 7.8.5* © 2000-2007 Rick Meyers. All rights reserved.

9 "International Standard Version," *e-Sword Version 7.8.5* © 2000-2007 Rick Meyers. All rights reserved.

10 "Strong's Hebrew and Greek Dictionaries," *e-Sword Version 7.8.5* © 2000-2007 Rick Meyers. All rights reserved.

11 "Strong's Hebrew and Greek Dictionaries," *e-Sword Version 7.8.5* © 2000-2007 Rick Meyers. All rights reserved.

12 "Strong's Hebrew and Greek Dictionaries," *e-Sword Version 7.8.5* © 2000-2007 Rick Meyers. All rights reserved.

13 "Strong's Hebrew and Greek Dictionaries," *e-Sword Version 7.8.5* © 2000-2007 Rick Meyers. All rights reserved.

14 "water," *Microsoft Encarta Encyclopedia 2000.* © 1993–1999 Microsoft Corporation. All rights reserved.

15 Kenneth Copeland Ministries

16 "light," *Microsoft Encarta Encyclopedia 2000.* © 1993–1999 Microsoft Corporation. All rights reserved.

17 "Atmosphere," *Microsoft Encarta Encyclopedia 2000.* © 1993–1999 Microsoft Corporation. All rights reserved.

18 "Photosynthesis," *Microsoft Encarta Encyclopedia 2000.* © 1993–1999 Microsoft Corporation. All rights reserved.

19 "Egg Cell," *Microsoft Encarta Encyclopedia 2000.* © 1993–1999 Microsoft Corporation. All rights reserved.

20 "Egg Cell," *Microsoft Encarta Encyclopedia 2000.* © 1993–1999 Microsoft Corporation. All rights reserved.

21 "1898 Young's Literal Translation," *e-Sword Version 7.8.5* © 2000-2007 Rick Meyers. All rights reserved.

21 "Genetics," *Microsoft Encarta Encyclopedia 2000.* © 1993–1999 Microsoft Corporation. All rights reserved.

23 "Strong's Hebrew and Greek Dictionaries," *e-Sword Version 7.8.5* © 2000-2007 Rick Meyers. All rights reserved.

24 "Strong's Hebrew and Greek Dictionaries," *e-Sword Version 7.8.5* © 2000-2007 Rick Meyers. All rights reserved.

25 "1833 Webster Bible," *e-Sword Version 7.8.5* © 2000-2007 Rick Meyers. All rights reserved.

26 "International Standard Version," *e-Sword Version 7.8.5* © 2000-2007 Rick Meyers. All rights reserved.

27 "Strong's Hebrew and Greek Dictionaries," *e-Sword Version 7.8.5* © 2000-2007 Rick Meyers. All rights reserved.

28 "Strong's Hebrew and Greek Dictionaries," *e-Sword Version 7.8.5* © 2000-2007 Rick Meyers. All rights reserved.

29 "Strong's Hebrew and Greek Dictionaries," *e-Sword Version 7.8.5* © 2000-2007 Rick Meyers. All rights reserved.

30 "Strong's Hebrew and Greek Dictionaries," *e-Sword Version 7.8.5* © 2000-2007 Rick Meyers. All rights reserved.

31 "Strong's Hebrew and Greek Dictionaries," *e-Sword Version 7.8.5* © 2000-2007 Rick Meyers. All rights reserved.

32 "Strong's Hebrew and Greek Dictionaries," *e-Sword Version 7.8.5* © 2000-2007 Rick Meyers. All rights reserved.

33 "Strong's Hebrew and Greek Dictionaries," *e-Sword Version 7.8.5* © 2000-2007 Rick Meyers. All rights reserved.

34 "Strong's Hebrew and Greek Dictionaries," *e-Sword Version 7.8.5* © 2000-2007 Rick Meyers. All rights reserved.

35 "1898 Young's Literal Translation," *e-Sword Version 7.8.5* © 2000-2007 Rick Meyers. All rights reserved.

36 "Strong's Hebrew and Greek Dictionaries," *e-Sword Version 7.8.5* © 2000-2007 Rick Meyers. All rights reserved.

37 "Strong's Hebrew and Greek Dictionaries," *e-Sword Version 7.8.5* © 2000-2007 Rick Meyers. All rights reserved.

38 "Strong's Hebrew and Greek Dictionaries," *e-Sword Version 7.8.5* © 2000-2007 Rick Meyers. All rights reserved.

39 "Strong's Hebrew and Greek Dictionaries," *e-Sword Version 7.8.5* © 2000-2007 Rick Meyers. All rights reserved.

40 "Easton's Bible Dictionary," *e-Sword Version 7.8.5* © 2000-2007 Rick Meyers. All rights reserved.

41 "Strong's Hebrew and Greek Dictionaries," *e-Sword Version 7.8.5* © 2000-2007 Rick Meyers. All rights reserved.

42 "Strong's Hebrew and Greek Dictionaries," *e-Sword Version 7.8.5* © 2000-2007 Rick Meyers. All rights reserved.

43 "Strong's Hebrew and Greek Dictionaries," *e-Sword Version 7.8.5* © 2000-2007 Rick Meyers. All rights reserved.

44 "Strong's Hebrew and Greek Dictionaries," *e-Sword Version 7.8.5* © 2000-2007 Rick Meyers. All rights reserved.

45 "Strong's Hebrew and Greek Dictionaries," *e-Sword Version 7.8.5* © 2000-2007 Rick Meyers. All rights reserved.

61 "Muhammad (prophet)," *Microsoft Encarta
   Encyclopedia 2000.* © 1993–1999 Microsoft
   Corporation. All rights reserved.
62 "Muhammad (prophet)," *Microsoft Encarta
   Encyclopedia 2000.* © 1993–1999 Microsoft
   Corporation. All rights reserved.

Printed in the United States
101822LV00002B/145-999/A

9 781604 771374